Black and White Balance

Black and White Balance

Matt Petryga

Petryga, Matt, author.
    Black and white balance / Matt Petryga.
    Vancouver, British Columbia: Matt Petryga, 2020.
ISBN: 978-1-7773199-0-8
LCSH Self-actualization (Psychology) | Dualism. | Motivation (Psychology) | Success--Psychological aspects. | Self-help techniques. | BISAC SELF-HELP / Personal Growth / Success | SELF-HELP / Motivational & Inspirational | PHILOSOPHY / General | PSYCHOLOGY / General
Classification: LCC BF637.S4 P4482 2020 | DDC 158--dc23

I dedicate this book to YOU

Table of Contents

Introduction
The Purpose Of This Book

Thank You. My deepest gratitude goes out to you for picking up this book. Whether you picked this book up from a bookstore, received it as a gift, or was given it from myself to you personally. I am joyous that it entered your life and that the material in this book may be used to enhance the quality of your unique world.

My name is Matt Petryga and I live in Vancouver, British Columbia, Canada.

The reason that I wrote this book is because I do not want to sell you a dream. Instead, I want to sell you on the idea that you can create a new reality for yourself. I have read countless Self-Help books from touchy-feely books, motivational books, business books, and step-by-step books. Most of these books sound good in theory, but they simply do not work. I wanted to create the ultimate Self-Help book that can help anybody in the world. I believe in practicality, non-conventional approaches, and methods that actually work and produce real world results.

I do not believe in normal or the ordinary. I only believe in the extraordinary. I believe that we all have extraordinary wired inside of us from the time we are born to the time that we leave this world. Extraordinary is inside each one of us and it is up to ourselves to bring out that extraordinary to live out a life of true extraordinaire. Expansion of growth in all areas of our life allows us to strive for and achieve mastery. Mastery of our life should be the goal.

When you read this book, I want you to keep in mind that applied knowledge is power. Knowledge alone will not help you. The greatest power in the world is useless if it is not applied. That is why I greatly encourage you to apply the knowledge in this book and you will see that your life will improve to new levels that you never could have imagined before.

This book will challenge you no matter what quality of life that you are currently living. This book will challenge you physically, psychologically, spiritually, and financially. This book will be in your face at times, it will make you emotional, and it will deliver the cold hard truth. All of the knowledge in this book works and has proven to work in my life time after time again. I have tried new concepts and have succeeded. I have tried new concepts and failed.

In this book, I share what has allowed me to achieve success in my life. I have read any major Self-Help book that you can think of and I have studied the pioneers of psychology. I have studied the highest performance athletes, musicians, scientists, religious leaders, business leaders, entrepreneurs, doctors, inventors, speakers, politicians, and the greatest minds of our time and of well before our time. I know why people do the things that they do and what their needs are. I believe that humans are complicated in a simple way and simple in a complicated way. Humans are not very hard to figure out once you understand their needs.

I have made it my duty to master my craft of high performance and to execute my life's purpose to influence people to live out their dreams. Success means different things for different people, but the basis for success is a simple formula. We over complicate everything. I do not believe in staying in the realm of complacency. I believe that you can always expand your horizons, you can always do more, you can always get better, and increase the quality of life that you live. If you were not meant to further develop yourself and that you "maxed out" on your potential, what would be the reason for you to keep living? Learning is a lifetime process and life in every way is truly multidimensional and unlimited. We are operating in so many dimensions that most people fail to realize that there is way more to our life than what meets the eye.

My ultimate goal for you as the reader is to implement the knowledge in this book to your personal life, whether you want to improve physically, mentally, psychologically, spiritually, financially, or in any other areas of your life that you feel needs refining. I want you to achieve the quality of life that you deserve to live. I want you to be healthier, happier, richer, loved, and greater spirited. I want all of the positive components that make a human achieve their full self-actualization a reality in your life. That is the whole reason why I developed this book from complete scratch.

My greatest gift is touching the life of someone else and making them look within themselves to realize that they can do anything in the world and that the only person that is stopping them is themselves. I do not care what your parents say, the government says, society says, your family says, your friends say, and anybody else on the planet. I know that you can have the world if you believe that it belongs to you and you are willing to pay the price to achieve your grandest goals and dreams. Everything in life has a price. It is all a matter of if you are willing to pay the price. How bad do you really want it? If you want it bad enough, it is yours and nobody is stopping you.

Forget society that has conditioned you to think otherwise. This is your story and your life. So start living it. I know this book will be of maximum value to you if you truly take the content of this book to heart and believe in a better version of yourself. That is all I want for you and that is all I want you to have for yourself too. Enjoy!

With great love,
—Matt Petryga

Black and White

This first chapter is going to be very unconventional, but it will be completely necessary for you to read every word. This chapter in will test your patience. Keep in mind that patience is a virtue that it is essential for you to have in order to succeed in anything that you do in life. I consider this chapter to be a healthy test of your patience. The concepts presented here will make sense to you later and will also help you to brainstorm your own ideas.

All of the words are going to be considered binary. However, the words will not be traditional binary symbols such as a series of zeros and ones, as in mathematics and digital electronics:

0011000000011000100110000001100010011000000110001001100
0100110001001100000011000000110001001100000011000100110
0000011000100110000001100010011000000110001001100000011000100110
1000100110000001100010011000000110001001100000110001001100
0110000001100010011000000110001001100000011000100110001100
0001100010011000000110001001100000011000000110000001100000110
0010011000000110001001100010011000100110001001100000011
0000001100000011000000110001001100000011000100110001100100
1100000001100010011000000110001001100010011000000110000
0011000100110000001100010011000000110001001100000110
01001100000011000000110001001100000011000101100010011000
0010011000000110001001100010011011000000110001001100000

We do not need to give meaning to any of these numbers. Instead, we can take a small fragment of the above numbers and convert them. Just take a single 0 and a single 1 from the above to form 01. Now give each number a meaning. 0 will be given the value of one extreme end and the 1 will be given the value of the opposite extreme end. The two numbers are now completely distanced from each other. They are completely sun and moon.

To give you an example, take moon and say that moon represents 0. Now take the sun and give the sun the value of 1. Now we are going to apply this concept. Every first word that I use will be the 0. Every second word that I use will be the 1. Please be patient and read every word. Note that the 0 could be 1 and the 1 could be 0.

Sun-Moon Lightness-Darkness Love-Hate Near-Far Coming-Going Give-Receive Heated-Unheated Successful-Unsuccessful Fast-Slow Skinny-Fat Big-Small Up-Down Left-Right Women-Men Past-Future Rich-Poor Mother-Father Fit-Unfit Employed-Unemployed Spending-Saving Buying-Selling Healthy-Unhealthy Ying-Yang Above-Below Absence-Presence Accept-Refuse Accidental-Intentional Active-Lazy Add-Subtract Admit-Deny Adult-Child Advanced-Elementary Affirmative-Negative Afraid-Brave After-Before Against-For Alike-Different Alive-Dead All-None Allow-Forbid Always-Never Ancient-Modern Ancestor-Descendant Agree-Disagree Amateur-Professional Amuse-Bore Angel-Devil Animal-Human Annoy-Satisfy Answer-Question Synonym-Antonym Apart-Together Approximately-Exactly Arrive-Depart Artificial-Natural Asleep-Awake Attack-Defend Attic-Cellar Spring-Winter Delicious-Awful Front-Back Background-Foreground Backward-Forward Good-Bad Lucky-Unlucky Beauty-Ugly Beginning-Ending Worst-Best Worse-Better Birth-Death Bitter-Sweet Bottom-Top Borrow-Lend Break-Fix Broad-Narrow Calm-Excited Careful-Careless Hit-Miss Ceiling-Floor Inner-Outer Certain-Uncertain Constant-Variable Cheap-Expensive Clean-Dirty Unclear-Clear Intelligent-Unintelligent

Close-Open Cold-Hot Simple-Complicated Insult-Compliment Consonant-Vowel Construction-Destruction Stop-Go True-False Correct-Wrong Create-Destroy Kind-Cruel Laugh-Cry Damage-Repair Dangerous-Safe Dawn-Dusk Day-Night Victory-Defeat Scarcity-Abundance Live-Die Easy-Hard Divide-Unite Divorce-Marry Domestic-Import Dry-Wet Early-Late East-West North-South Empty-Full Enemy-Friend Entrance-Exit Everybody-Nobody Odd-Even Everything-Nothing Shelter-Exposure Extreme-Moderate Fail-Succeed Start-Finish Flat-Round Native-Foreigner Freeze-Unfreeze Frequently-Occasionally New-Old Serious-Unserious Generous-Ungenerous Gentle-Rough Giant-Tiny Host-Guest Guilty-Innocent Happiness-Sadness Plant-Harvest Heaven-Hell Light-Heavy Here-There Ours-Yours Vertical-Horizontal Husband-Wife Ignore-Notice In-Out Inside-Outside Interested-Uninterested Action-Reaction Junior-Senior Learn-Teach Lead-Follow Less-More Solid-Liquid Long-Short Lose-Win Low-High Lower-Raise Major-Minor Some-Many Noon-Midnight Little-Much Yes-No Noisy-Silent Now-Then Vacant-Occupied Off-On Ordinary-Extraordinary Over-Under Part-Whole Peace-War Polite-Rude Wealth-Poverty Private-Public Pull-Push Sunny-Rainy Remember-Forget Rise-Sink Salt-Sugar Scream-Whisper Seldom-Often Separate-Connect Servant-Master Deep-Shallow Single-Multiple Sit-Stand Stranger-Familiar Strong-Weak Alpha-Beta Hungry-Thirsty literate-Illiterate Yesterday-Tomorrow Useful-Useless Young-Old Accurate-Inaccurate Advantage-Disadvantage Attract-Repulse Bless-Curse Straight-Crooked Blame-Praise Limited-Unlimited Conceal-Reveal Cool-Warm Clockwise-Counterclockwise Common-Rare Contract-Expand Captive-Free Increase-Decrease Encourage-Discourage Interior-Exterior Lost-Found Fresh-Stale Fortunate-Unfortunate Grow-Shrink Help-Hinder Protagonist-Antagonist Pro-Anti Honest-Dishonest Superior-Inferior Inhale-Exhale Important-Trivial Justice-Injustice Just-Unjust Known-Unknown Landlord-Tenant First-Last Legal-Illegal Likely-Unlikely Lenient-Strict Lose-Find Loyal-Disloyal

Maximum-Minimum Mature-Immature Understand-Misunderstand Nadir-Zenith Obedient-Disobedient Optimist-Pessimist Famous-Infamous Pure-Impure Temporary-Permanent Singular-Plural Patient-Impatient Poetry-Prose Impossible-Possible Prudent-Imprudent Qualified-Unqualified Regular-Irregular Same-Opposite Satisfactory-Unsatisfactory Secure-Insecure Collect-Scatter Reap-Sow Intoxicated-Sober Opaque-Transparent Vanish-Appear Virtue-Vice Voluntary-Compulsory Visible-Invisible Wise-Unwise Perfect-Imperfect Black-White.

As you can imagine, there are an endless amount of opposites in the world. The purpose of reading all those words was for you to recognize that everything in life is either on one end of the spectrum or on the other end of the spectrum. This is important to know because if you are doing something about your situation or not doing something about your situation, you are on one side or the on other side. In the simplest form, this is true about anything in life. Are you talking about something? Or are you actually doing the thing that you are talking about? I want you to be honest with yourself and to ask yourself and to think about your life for a moment. I want you to think about your goal, dream, or whatever it is that you are trying to achieve in this life.

Ask yourself, "Am I doing everything that I possibly can to fulfill my goal?" Or "Can I be working harder on my goal than I already am?" It is that simple. It is completely mind blowing to see people not asking themselves a simple question. Are they on the black or are they on the white? Are they on the 0? Or are they on the 1? The problem lies in the fact that people are not honest with themselves. Anytime you grow, try a new activity, or experiment with a new idea, it will cause moderate to extreme discomfort.

The reason for this is because when we do not know what to expect and are not used to something, we create anxiety in ourselves by nature. You need to break out of your box and try anyway. People will almost always do more to avoid discomfort than they will do to possibly reap the rewards of doing something that will bring a lot of joy to them. People mentally block their mind with self-limiting beliefs and do not allow themselves to trust that they are able to achieve anything that they put their mind to.

It is such a simple question. So ask yourself, what side of the spectrum are you on? What side of the spectrum do you want to be on? A spectrum has one extreme end or the other extreme end. You have a decision to make and it is better to go with the decision that will help you in the long run than the decision that will only help you in the short term. People give up way too easily and do not realize that the best things in life are the things that are going to take a much longer period of time to achieve. You should go into executing your goal by getting excited to do short runs, because enough short runs will eventually equal a long run.

Get excited to complete the first thing that you have to do, then have that exact same energy to complete the second thing that you have to do, then continue until you are at the finish line. If we get excited momentarily and give up at the half way, or worse, before, what is the point of going for it if you are not going to follow through with your thoughts all the way? Keep in mind that for everything positive, there is something negative to counterbalance it.

Are you as wealthy as you want to be? Are you not as wealthy as you want to be?

Are you as fit as you want to be? Are you not as fit as you want to be?

Are you as healthy as you want to be? Are you not as healthy as you want to be?

Are you in the best job that you want to be in? Are you not in the best job that you want to be in?

Are you in the happiest marriage that you want to be in? Are you not in the happiest marriage that you want to be in?

Are you in the happiest relationship that you want to be in? Are you not in the happiest relationship that you want to be in?

Are you the person that you want to be? Are you not the person that you want to be?

Are you being honest with yourself? Are you not being honest with yourself?

Are you doing the best that you can? Are you not doing the best that you can?

Are you a good business partner? Are you not a good business partner?

Are you worried about the future? Are you not worried about the future?

Are you stuck in the past? Are you not stuck in the past?

Are you eating the right foods? Are you not eating the right foods?

Are you exercising? Are you not exercising?

Are you selling? Are you not selling?

Are you negotiating from a place of strength? Are you not negotiating from a place of strength?

Are you knowledgeable on a subject? Are you not knowledgeable on a subject?

Are you respected? Are you not respected?

Are you independent? Are you not independent?

Are you enjoying the way that things are going? Are you not enjoying the way that things are going?

Are you making something a priority? Are you not making something a priority?

Are you getting up early everyday? Are you not getting up early everyday?

Are you being lazy? Are you not being lazy?

Are you procrastinating? Are you not procrastinating?

Are you being taken advantage of? Are you not being taken advantage of?

Are you controlling your life? Are you not controlling your life?

Are you taking action? Are you not taking action?

Are you working to make yourself a better person? Are you not working to make yourself a better person?

Are you allowing yourself to have fun? Are you not allowing yourself to have fun?

Are you giving yourself excuses? Are you not giving yourself excuses?

Are you allowing self-doubt to dictate your life? Are you not allowing self-doubt to dictate your life?

Are you taking something seriously? Are you not taking something seriously?

Are you allowing yourself to be open minded? Are you not allowing yourself to be open minded?

Are you able to forgive? Are you not able to forgive?

Are you going to stand up for yourself? Are you not going to stand up for yourself?

Are you going to face your fear or your fears? Are you not going to face your fear or your fears?

Are you going to try something new? Are you not going to try something new?

Are you going to show gratitude? Are you not going to show gratitude?

Are you going to be successful? Are you not going to be successful?

Are you going to believe something that you told your self? Are you not going to believe something that you told yourself?

Are you going to believe something someone else said about you? Are you not going to believe something someone else said about you?

Are you going to create a system? Are you not going to create a system?

Are you going to dress nicely? Are you not going to dress nicely?

Are you going to accept failure? Are you not going to accept failure?

Are you going to believe in luck? Are you not going to believe in luck?

Are you going to get abused? Are you not going to get abused?

Are you living your dreams? Are you not living your dreams?

Are you going to stand up for someone else? Are you not going to stand up for someone else?

Are you going to allow yourself to be jealous? Are you not going to allow yourself to be jealous?

Are you going to believe in yourself? Are you not going to believe in yourself?

Are you going to believe in something? Are you not going to believe in something?

Are you going to allow your addiction to continue? Are you not going to allow your addiction to continue?

Are you going to read more? Are you not going to read more?

Are you going to save your money? Are you not going to save your money?

Are you going to act on impulse? Are you not going to act on impulse?

Are you going to spend more time being productive? Are you not going to spend more time being productive?

Are you going to limit your usage of social media? Are you not going to limit your usage of social media?

Are you going to spend more time on the phone? Are you not going to spend more time on the phone?

Are you going to be happy? Are you not going to be happy?

Are you going to be sad? Are you not going to be sad?

Are you going to be a leader? Are you not going to be a leader?

Are you going to learn more about something? Are you not going to learn more about something?

Are you going to spend more time practicing? Are you mot going to spend more time practicing?

Are you going to document something? Are you not going to document something?

Are you going to do a blog? Are you not going to do a blog?

Are you going to get a new wardrobe? Are you not going to get a new wardrobe?

Are you going to live a new life? Are you not going to live a new life?

Are you going to accept change? Are you not going to accept change?

Are you going to adapt to your environment? Are you not going to adapt to your environment?

Are you going to allow yourself to remain in poverty? Are you not going to allow yourself to remain in poverty?

Are you going to leave a situation? Are you not going to leave a situation?

Are you going to write a book? Are you not going to write a book?

Are you going to try again? Are you not going to try again?

Are you going to say no? Are you not going to say no?

Are you going to say yes? Are you not going to say yes?

Are you going to change your life? Are you not going to change your life?

Are you going to apply the Black and White Balance principles in your life? Are you not going to apply the Black and White Balance Principles in your life?

Are you going to die happy? Are you not going to die happy?

There is an endless amount of questions that you can ask yourself. You will always have two questions and ultimately one decision to decide for yourself. The idea is so simple and basic. It really does not matter who you are, where you come form, or what your beliefs are, the decision making between two questions will always be true. It never changes.

One thing that you may find effective in making a new decision is to record through video or audio you asking yourself your two questions and calculate the better, more positive decision. Once you have formulated the two questions and decided which statement to go with, the next step would be to take action. Whatever you decided, do not second guess yourself and go with your gut instinct.

If your two questions to yourself were, "Do I want to be wealthier?" "Do I not want to be wealthier?" confidently make up your mind and say, "I do want to be wealthier" and take action without any doubts in your mind. You know the right answer and the more positive answer deep down within. We all know the answer deep within ourselves. The problem is that we talk or think ourselves out of doing something or we only half commit to something. We must believe in our self, get rid of the doubts, and fully commit to whatever it is that we need to commit to.

I have mentioned the word "You" frequently already in the book. The reason I use the word "You" so frequently, is because it really is that simple.

You, You, You, You, You, You, You, You, You, You, You, You,
You, You, You, You, You, You, You, You, You, You, You, You,
You, You, You, You, You, You, You, You, You, You, You, You,
You, You, You, You, You, You, You, You, You, You, You, You,
You, You, You, You, You, You, You, You, You, You, You, You,
You, You, You, You, You, You, You, You, You, You, You, You,
You, You, You, You, You, You, You, You, You, You, You, You,
You, You, You, You, You, You, You, You, You, You, You, You,
You, You, You, You, You, You, You, You, You, You, You, You,
You, You, You, You, You, You, You, You, You, You, You, You,
You, You, You, You, You, You, You, You, You, You, You, You,
You, You, You, You, You, You, You, You, You, You, You, You,
You, You, You, You, You, You, You, You, You, You, You, You,
You, You, You, You, You, You, You, You, You, You, You, You,
You, You, You, You, You, You, You, You, You, You, You, You,
You, You, You, You, You, You, You, You, You, You, You, You,
You, You, You, You, You, You, You, You, You, You, You, You,
You, You, You, You, You, You, You, You, You, You, You, You,
You, You, You, You, You, You, You, You, You, You, You, You,
You, You, You, You, You, You, You, You, You, You, You, You,
You, You, You, You, You, You, You, You, You, You, You, You,
You, You, You, You, You, You, You, You, You, You, You, You,
You, You, You, You, You, You, You, You, You, You, You, You,
You, You, You, You, You, You, You, You, You, You, You, You,
You, You, You, You, You, You, You, You, You, You, You, You,
You, You, You, You, You, You, You, You, You, You, You, You,
You, You, You, You, You, You, You, You, You, You, You, You,

You, You, You, You, You, You, You, You, You, You, You, You,
You, You, You, You, You, You, You, You, You, You, You, You,
You, You, You, You, You, You, You, You, You, You, You, You,
You, You, You, You, You, You, You, You, You, You, You, You,
You, You, You, You, You, You, You, You, You, You, You, You,
You, You, You, You, You, You, You, You, You, You, You, You,
You, You, You, You, You, You, You, You, You, You, You, You,
You, You, You, You, You, You, You, You, You, You, You, You,
You, You, You, You, You, You, You, You, You, You, You, You,
You, You, You, You, You, You, You, You, You, You, You, You,
You, You, You, You, You, You, You, You, You, You, You, You,
You, You, You, You, You, You, You, You, You, You, You, You,
You, You, You, You, You, You, You, You, You, You, You, You,
You, You, You, You, You, You, You, You, You, You, You, You,
You, You, You, You, You, You, You, You, You, You, You, You,
You, You, You, You, You, You, You, You, You, You, You, You,
You, You, You, You, You, You, You, You, You, You, You, You,
You, You, You, You, You, You, You, You, You, You, You, You,
You, You, You, You, You, You, You, You, You, You, You, You,
You, You, You, You, You, You, You, You, You, You, You, You,
You, You, You, You, You, You, You, You, You, You, You, You,
You, You, You, You, You, You, You, You, You, You, You, You,
You, You, You, You, You, You, You, You, You, You, You, You,
You, You, You, You, You, You, You, You, You, You, You, You,
You, You, You, You, You, You, You, You, You, You, You, You,
You, You, You, You, You, You, You, You, You, You, You, You,
You, You, You, You, You, You, You, You, You, You, You, You,
You, You, You, You, You, You, You, You, You, You, You, You,
You, You, You, You, You, You, You, You, You, You, You, You,
You, You, You, You, You, You, You, You, You, You, You, You,
You, You, You, You, You, You, You, You, You, You, You, You,
You, You, You, You, You, You, You, You, You, You, You, You,
You, You, You, You, You, You, You, You, You, You, You, You,
You, You, You, You, You, You, You, You, You, You, You, You,
You, You, You, You, You, You, You, You, You, You, You, You.

Everything in this entire life starts with you and ends with you. Take a blank painting canvas and paint the word "You". It does not matter what color you paint it. Take that painting and hang it up in your room to look at it every single day for the rest of your life. People do not want to take responsibility for their life. They do not want to put in the time, energy, and work. People want something miraculous to suddenly show up at their door and they wait their entire lives for something to show up. Well it does not and it will not ever happen that way.

If you were to type anything in existence on the computer, an image would pop up of the exact thing that you thought of. If you can see a picture of it on the computer, you can have it in your life. If your life ended, you would be the one that ended, not anything else. I just want you to have the idea of you in your head. Do not give yourself the excuse of being selfish. You are actually being selfish by not allowing yourself to focus on building your best possible life.

If you cannot love yourself, then how can anyone possibly love you to the fullest potential? I am not saying to be conceited and to hurt people, but what I am saying is to allow yourself to invest the time, resources, and action in your life. If I were to rewrite this whole entire book in one single word, that one single word would be "You". You are the one with the answers. You are the one with the decisions to make. You are the one that needs to take the proper action. You are the one that needs to experience the excitement and fulfillment of successfully completing your goals, dreams, and purpose.

Nobody else can get you there except for you. There is no use for you when you are dead so you better make use of yourself while you are still alive. When you are dead, all the people that ever laughed at you, doubted you, or did not believe in you will also be dead. Nothing will matter when you are dead so you may as well make the best of it while you are still here. If you really comprehended the idea of how little time we actually have on this planet, it would move you. We are here for only a short time, and the odds of us being here today are 1 in 400,000,000,000,000. That number again is one in four hundred trillion.

If you really understood the odds of your entire existence, it would move you so hard that you would live each and everyday to the absolute fullest like it is your last. The accomplishments that you would achieve knowing the odds would be unbelievable. Your sperm cell was the one that fertilized the egg out of the millions of sperm cells that did not. If your parents had sex with each other even a millisecond earlier, or a millisecond later, you may not even exist right now. I know that sounds graphic, but it is the complete and utter truth. Those giant numbers that were mentioned makes it obvious that there is something much more spiritual about life than we really know.

It is important to live each and every one of your days in a meaningful way. Use all the talent, creativity, and gifts that you were given and let those qualities shine as life intended. All of this sounds incredibly deep but I want it to hit you so that it awakens something inside of you. I want it to hit you right into your unconsciousness and spirit that you lose your mind and decide to do something about your life. I do not want you to suffer any more and I want you to live this great and beautiful life to the maximum potential that it was designed for you to live. You only deserve the best life because it is your birthright. The fact that we have bad days indicates that we are not maximizing all the potential that we deserve to experience. Everyone deserves the divine life that each and every one of us has been granted.

The only catch to this is that you have to live by putting your full efforts into life. You have to give it your all. Then it will hit you so hard that you will not even see it coming when you are living your purpose. You will not feel as if you are in reality anymore. You will feel a bright paradise on this dark universe. I cannot even put into words the sensation that you will feel once you have gotten to that place. Your life will feel as if you are living in a movie where you are the star actor in this world.

Everything will be going in ways that you could not even dream of. It only requires you to work hard and put the time in.

Learn, grow, develop, pursue. The whole world is waiting for you to jump out from behind the curtains and perform. Butterflies will fluctuate throughout your entire stomach, your soul will be lifted, and you will feel reborn. You will not experience pain when you are in that place. I really want you to get there for yourself. Please just do you and beat that devil on your shoulder robbing you of your dreams. Follow the angel that tells you that you can have it all.

If you could have anything in the entire world more than anything, what would it be? Whatever your answer is, I want you to do that, act on that, and do nothing else but that. Just pursue that. Do not let anything or anyone get in your way. It will happen and when it does, you will feel your spirit and soul begin to shine into a wonderful world that you never knew existed before. I promise you. Even when I promise you, it is about you. The promise that I make is about you and only you.

I hope to inspire you to allow yourself to try new things. When you do the things that you do not normally do and allow yourself to explore possibilities, it completely opens up your mind. You need to engage your mind as much as you can because when your mind is engaged, your life will also be engaged. Sometimes you may think to yourself that there is nothing else for you to do and that is completely untrue. If life had nothing else in store for you, you would have been dead a long time ago. As long as you are alive, you have a purpose to fulfill.

If you think of an explosive or bomb, it starts off by being ignited and the blast wave creates highly compressed air particles. Next, shockwaves carry through the medium, and fragmentation (Which means the air particles break into smaller, separate parts) throws shrapnel (Which is fragments of the bomb being thrown out by the explosion) the explosion creates a mixture of heat and fire, which causes a shock wave to travel rapidly away from its core. The idea is that a shockwave cannot travel any distance if the bomb is not ignited. The same is true with your life.

You need to start small before you can scale anything to a great size. Always start small, no matter what it is that you do in life, especially if it is something new. Always take one step forward in the right direction of the goal even if that means that you only take a baby step at a time. One step closer to your final goal is one step closer to completing your goal. You could think of it as planting the bombs of your life, your goals being the bomb. The distance of the shockwave from the explosion would be considered the progress that you have made since the explosion happened. We all have the bombs of our life, we just need to plant it and have faith that our bomb will create a successful explosion. You know who sets the fire to the bombs in your life? You set the fire to the bombs in your life.

By now, you should realize that you cannot do anything in life if you simply do not allow yourself to do it. Nobody is pressuring you to live a better life, not even me. The way to go about things is to give yourself pressure to complete your goals. If there is no pressure fueling you to get something done, you will not do it. The best pressure in life is setting a date for when it should be done. If something you want takes a month to complete, put the last day of the month as "Goal needs to be completed."

That is a great start, but even that alone may not help you as effectively as it should. "Goal needs to be completed" as the last day of the month needs to be followed up by weekly goals and may also include daily goals. If on the 7th day of the first week of the month you say, "Goal needs to be one quarter completed by today" then you put for the 14th day of the second week "Goal needs to be one half done". Then on the 21st day of the third week you can say "Goal needs to be three fourths done" and then on the 28th day of the last week you can put "Goal needs to be completed fully today".

Do you see how powerful it is to pressure yourself in a positive manner? If you do not see how powerful this is, apply it to your life and see how much more you are able to achieve. Like I've said before, later never comes. Later is the worst excuse of humankind. Do it now. If you can have daily goals, it will be the most effective way to execute more action. If you only put "Goal needs to be completed fully today" on the last day of the month, it will potentially allow you to procrastinate and put it off because you feel that you still have lots of time. The next thing you know, it is two days before "Time is up" and you have not even started your goal. The more pressure that you put on yourself, the better. Keep in mind though that some things in life are simply unrealistic to complete in one day.

Do not completely overwhelm yourself and bite off more than you can chew. When people are way too overwhelmed, they may do nothing about it because of the anxiety. Set realistic goals. If you think about school, the people that study daily usually do better on the test deadline compared to the people that cram everything and study the night before the test. Without the proper preparation, I guarantee that you will fail. In school, whoever would complete projects on time usually gets higher marks than people that bring in their assignments late. The smart kids are not necessarily smarter, but they do have the right time management and are able to put healthy stress on themselves in an effective way in order to achieve success. The smartest kid in the class will fail a test if they do not study and manage their time properly. If the most unintelligent kid in the class studies hard everyday, with the right help and time management, that kid will succeed. Hard work and dedication beats talent every single time. The only way to truly be dedicated and to put in the right energy is to manage your time.

Along with the proper time management, you need to communicate to the world properly. It is one thing to have a goal, and it is completely another thing to have completed the goal. Saying that you are going to do something and then doing nothing about it is a terrible way to communicate to the world. In fact, it is not communicating to the world at all. Not in a single way, shape, or form. You may as well go to sleep because it does not mean a single thing. What you need to be doing is asking what you want, believing in it, then doing it. The world listens 90% to your actions and only 10% to what you think in your head. The 10% is your vision and visions are formed through your thoughts. The 90% is the action to turn your visions into reality. If the world sees you working on your goal and actively doing what you are thinking, it will listen to you every single time without failure. When your actions are equal to your thoughts, the world will perk up and help you to gain the resources needed to complete the project that you are trying to achieve.

Since we are already talking about binary numbers, I want to share another way to look at numbers.

-1047296, -523648, -261824, -130912, -65456, -32728, -16364, -8192, -4096, -2048 -1024, -512, -256, -128, -64, -32, -16, -8, -4, -2, -1
-0
0
+0
1,2,4,8,16,32,64,128,256,512,1024,2048,4096,8192,16364,3272 8,65456,130912, 261824,523648,1047296

The numbers doubled from an incredibly negative number to an incredibly positive number. This is a critical piece of information that you need to know because that is a mathematical law of the world. This information can help you in your business or to make extra money.

If you can figure how to get from $1 to $2, $2 to $4, $4 to $8, you have got it made. If you make $3,000 a month, double it. Of course this is easier said than done. However, if you think that $6,000 a month is double, you automatically increase the likelihood of you making that amount. The reason for this is because if you can think something, you can do it. Everything takes work but you need to have a thought before something is able to be a part of reality. If you want to increase the amount of followers on your social network site, or to earn new customers/clients, you need to be thinking in numbers. The best ways to be thinking in numbers is to double, triple, or quadruple them. When you allow yourself to think in numbers, you allow yourself to make much more calculated decisions. I am not saying to be a mathematician, I am simply stating that you have to understand basic math and you can use that math with a calculator.

You can think in emotional math too. For example, if you continue doing something that you do not like for a week, imagine how you will feel in two weeks time, and from two weeks time, in four weeks time. You will most likely be very upset continuing to allow yourself to do something that will emotionally hurt you in the long run. Calculate your emotions like you would calculate your finances. Things are only going to be negative or positive. If it is not going up, it is going down. If it is not growing, it is dying. When you are able to think about the long run, you are able to make much more calculated decisions. Everything needs to be able to scale and the best way to scale something is through doubling numbers.

Let's say that you have a staggering amount of debt in your life. Say the balance is $50,000. Think about how you are going to get from -$50,000 to -$25,000 and only focus on that. If you try and focus on the whole outstanding balance, you will tell yourself that it is impossible to achieve. When you are able to break things down into smaller pieces, then you are able to chew the pieces. If you try to consume something that is way too big to eat, you will not be able to eat it, or worse, you will choke. As mentioned before, it is much better to take small steps towards your goals than no steps at all.

For every achievement that you complete in life, the mathematical laws of nature will give you the opportunity to double those achievements. If you complete one achievement, two achievements that you can complete will emerge. Once you complete the new two achievements, then four achievements will emerge for you to have the opportunity to complete. Things are always going to double positively, or they are going to double negatively. It is much better in most cases to think about doubling positively.

Positive doubling attracts positive doubling and like attracts like. Think about a rich and successful celebrity and remember that rich breeds rich and fame breeds fame. If a rich celebrity was to endorse your product or hangout with you, you would probably have more of your products purchased and sales would increase. People would naturally know who you are all of a sudden because they have seen you with someone that has a tremendous amount of social proof. Therefore, you would reap the benefits because everything doubles based on what it is. One tree seed will be able to create many trees. One decision that you may make in your life could be the one that influences many other decisions that you will have to make in your life. One decision could change the whole course of your life for the better, or for the worse.

Everything is Black and White. You are either on the 0 or the 1. If you are standing on one side, how do you get to the other side? Are you on the side that you want to be on? When you start becoming self aware, you can make the correct decisions and actions to get on the side that you want to be on. One side or the other, it is that simple. Yes or No. Are you doing what you are thinking or are you not? Many people do not consciously think about what side they are on or they will procrastinate about going to the other side. If you understand that you are doing 0 about your life or you are doing 1 about your life, you will live differently. When you change your habits, you can change the side that you are on.

Numbers are the most important tangible measuring units that us humans have available. The more that you know about numbers and calculated risks, the better the quality of your life will be. Math is one of those things in this society that everybody seems to hate or strongly dislike. Math is simple once you understand the formula. Math never changes because no matter what you calculate, the answer will always be the same every time. Learn to love math because we live in a mathematical universe. How much alcohol by volume or what proof? The reason that people ask that is because we want to know and to accurately calculate the potency of a drink. Humans are very mathematically inclined, however, humans fail to use math as much as they should be using math. How long? How much time? How old? How often? How frequently? How much? How little? All of those questions are inquiring about a certain number because humans logically think in terms of numbers.

People will generally buy when they are less calculated and more emotionally stimulated by the idea of the product or service. People will purchase an expensive car because of the emotional appeal of the car rather than the logical part of their brain that thinks in numbers. This is important if you are a sales person. If you can make someone emotionally feel greater about your product or service than his or her mathematical logic and reason, they are more likely to purchase from you. When we are emotional, we tend to make decisions on feeling as opposed to an educated decision. So knowing that the world is mathematical, would it make sense to learn more about numbers? My theory is that if you do not apply more math and make proper calculations in your decision-making in this mathematical universe, the mathematical universe will calculate your life in ways that you may not want it to calculate. It is daunting to learn math and apply it, but the more that you apply math to your decision-making, the sounder your decision-making will be.

The banks are a prime example of decision-making. The banks will not loan you any money on emotion. The bank will only loan you money based on if something mathematically works. If you want to take out a loan, the bank assesses your ability to pay back the loan. The bank will determine if you are able to pay them back or not based on how much you make, your credit, and other variables. If the bank mathematically decides that you are a risk or that you may not be able to repay the loan in a reasonable amount of time, they simple will not loan to you. That is the mathematical decision making that you need to be able to generate in all aspects of your life. It does not matter if the mathematical decision-making is financial, emotional, or any other measurable patterns. When you can develop a systematic approach to your decisions, it will create such a momentum for you to have a happier life.

When you start to apply the practice of your numbers into every decision that you make, you start to make better decisions, but beware of your emotional state. Emotional decisions can be great and they can be disastrous. Good or bad, binary. The best decision makers can incredibly suffer if emotion gets in the way of your calculations. Imagine driving down the highway, all of a sudden there is heavy fog present. Lets say that the fog impairs your ability to see what is in front of you and you start to slow down. Emotions do the same thing to humans. Emotions impair us in making good decisions. When you are emotional, your sense of logic and reasoning starts to fall. That is why it is important to keep your emotions in check. The perfect binary example is either you are currently emotional or you are not currently emotional. This is essential for being mathematical. When we are feeling sad, depressed, angry, jealous, we tend to make impulsive conclusions and decisions based on the current emotional state. When we are not emotional, we are calm and able to make better decisions. Clear the fog out of your life when you need to make important decisions.

The way to practice better decision-making is hard thing, but it is necessary. It is binary, control your emotions or do not control your emotions. I am not telling you to become a robot, but when you masterfully control the state of your emotions, you can excel your life in a newfound way. The problem is that humans are very emotional. That is great and it is also not so great. Most people let their emotions control their whole life. People live day to day and only make decisions on how they are feeling and what their emotional state is. I am sure that you can see what may be dangerous about this approach to life. This is going to take a lot of practice, time, and patience, but I want you to learn how to control your emotions. Most people are simply conditioned to feel a certain way because it is comfortable for them. I am suggesting that you get out of your comfort zone and take your emotions out of your decision-making. Recognize when you are feeling the way that you feel. Recognize when you are making a decision that will affect the future. I want you to still be emotional and human because it is a beautiful thing, but if you are going to be going after your dreams, you need to take the calculated steps. Keep in mind that you do not need a perfect calculation, but a great estimate. Do not think too little about your decision and do not think too long about your decision, make the decision.

Do not tell yourself that something is hard, because if you believe that it is hard, it will be hard. Tell yourself that it is easy and it will become easier. Switch from one side of thinking to another. Tell yourself, "I am making emotional decisions right now and it is time to flip the switch and to make unemotional decisions." Instantly you changed sides all by becoming aware of what is around you and by recognizing the quality of your thoughts. You and only you can change your side for anything instantly. You will surprise yourself how simple it is to just start doing the opposite of what you are currently doing because everybody knows how to do the opposite of what they are currently doing. If you are able to flip the switch in anything that you do because of your emotional stability, you will never be the same. You will be a much more evolved version of yourself. When you evolve your self, your life will begin to evolve. When your life evolves, the people and environment around you start to evolve. When the people and environment around you start to evolve, that is when your life takes on a whole new meaning. You start to create the momentum for yourself to further progress rapidly towards your purpose, goals, dreams, and desires.

Evolve or devolve. That is your binary choice for you to make. Do I want to evolve my life into a better, newer version of myself? Or do I want to remain comfortable and not to step out of my comfort zone to achieve a greater version of myself? The choice is always going to be your choice. Nobody else has the power to make choices for you in your life. Do you want to be a 1 (something) or do you want to be a 0 (nothing). The greatest way to evolve your self is to work on yourself. Actively seek to learn new skills, new concepts, new ideas, and new beliefs. Grow in any way, shape, or form. The greatest way to devolve your self is to do absolutely nothing.

You have all of the control in the world to evolve yourself. You are going to be uncomfortable and fearful doing new things, but it will be worth it. Do not fear change and being uncomfortable. Evolution in life is the result of the complete and utter destruction of a past form. To evolve forward is to build from the previous. Humans are creatures of habit and habit causes us to not want to change because we are comfortable and secure. Humans are scared to change, but I think that it is more the fear of the process to change than the actual change. Humans naturally do not like the process of changing, but once they have changed, they tend to like the outcome result of the change.

When you first learn to ride a bike, you will fall down. Get up, try again, and fall again. Keep getting up until you learn how to ride the bike without falling. Once you are able to learn how to ride the bike without falling, you will have the biggest smile on your face and joy that you went through all of the discomfort to learn the new skill. The beauty about this is once you undergo all the discomfort and then you acquire the skill, you will have the new skill for the rest of your life. Everything in life is like that. Go through the bad and the goodness will pour. The effect is the exact same as going through the storm before the rainbow. All you have to do is to prepare yourself for the storm and get through it. Every storm eventually subsides and goes away, but the rainbow will be forever.

Think about the idea of everything being the same and never evolving. What would be the point of things not developing? Every day, there are advancements in technology, health, business, environment, knowledge, and anything that you could possibly think of. So if everything around you is progressing and evolving, why aren't you? Life is about growth and if you are not growing, you are dying. Growing and dying are completely binary. Expand your horizons and look deep within yourself to find the answers on how you can develop yourself physically, mentally, psychologically, emotionally, spiritually, sexually, whatever it may be.

With evolution, here is something that people really do not ever think about.

If everything went according to plan, exactly the way that you planned it, what would be the point? It would be a perfect world and anything perfect does not have the capacity to evolve. It is the imperfections of the plan that allows you to learn, grow, and evolve. How could you possibly grow if everything went perfectly planned? Life would be very dull and uninteresting. The charm and appeal of life is to live it with a sense of mystery. When things are not going as planned, you will learn so much more and appreciate the lessons of the unexpected outcomes. You will see the universal law of math come out into existence and you will appreciate more why things did not go a certain way.

When something does not go the way that you planned, you have to recalculate and try a new strategy until you get the desired outcome. It is not because the world is cruel, but it is simply a miscalculation on your end. Nobody on this planet has the mathematical capacity to plan and achieve the desired outcomes every time. The harder and more advanced the plan, the more calculations that are going to be required to execute the plan correctly. It all comes back to allowing your self to be patient and enjoying the process of completing the project. Patience is one of the most effective skills that you can possibly possess and practice. Especially when you do not have the necessary resources to complete a project, it will require you to become even more patient. To help yourself practice patience, just take one step at a time. Always look for the next step that you can take, even if that means taking a smaller step. Ten smaller steps are greater than one big step.

People always worry about what other people are thinking about them and some people try to please everybody. Well here is a binary for you that you need to digest in your life. People are going to like you or they are not going to like you. You simply cannot please everybody. Most people are not going to like you and that is completely okay. Do not even worry about the people that do not like you, if they cannot find the beauty in you, then they are not looking hard enough. Odds are that if they do not like you, they probably do not even like themselves. I know that may sound odd or hard to believe, but it is important to understand that hurt people hurt other people.

One binary that is essential to maintain your wellness is something that people do not think much about. That binary is sleep. Are you getting enough sleep every night? Or are you depriving yourself of adequate sleep? I cannot stress to you enough about how important it is to get your proper rest. Your body is an organ and it best functions when it is properly charged. If a battery is not charged, it will not work as well as if it is charged or it may not work at all. Your body is a battery and you must always make sure that it is charged. There is a myth that if you want to be really successful, you have to sacrifice sleep in order to achieve the level of success. If you want to be successful and live a healthy and Balanced life, you need your proper rest.

There are so many health complications that can arise of you abusing and wearing out your body over an extended period of time. To be successful and to maintain success, you must be at your best every day. There is no way that you are going to be able to perform at an optimal level if your mind is not completely concentrated on the goal that you are trying to achieve. If you think that sleep is not important, then keep yourself up for two days straight and see how functional you are. You will quickly learn that sleep is needed for your organs and your mind to work properly and effectively. Lots of people lack sleep progressively from day in and day out of work that they usually start to become less productive.

Your body has a natural system called a circadian rhythm, which is your body's twenty-four hour clock. This internal clock is continuously running in the background of your brain and it cycles between sleepiness and alertness at a consistent interval. It is valuable knowledge to learn about circadian rhythm because the more that you know about your body, the better that you can run it. So because of circadian rhythm, it is important that you do not alter the rhythm. That means that you should go to bed at the same time and get up at the same time for your peak performance. Of course that you knew sleep was important, but it is a lot more important than you think it is. Your brain cells need you to rest as well because if you do not sleep, your brain cells will begin to die. It is a scary thought, but it is reality. You are fully in control of your body if you learn and understand how to take care of it properly. Of course you have to apply the knowledge. There is no substitution for sleep. Are you getting enough proper sleep? Or are you not getting enough proper sleep? Take charge of your health.

Although learning is a very important thing that you should be actively doing every day, not everything that you learn is optimal for you to know and to apply in your life. You can do a lot of things, but not everything is great to do. This binary is one that is a lot harder to track, but it is important to develop the necessary radar for you to learn to eliminate redundant information and knowledge. Is what you are learning optimal for you to enhance your life and to achieve greater success? Or is what you are learning not optimal for you to enhance your life and to achieve greater success?

The truth is, a lot of people place high emphasis on learning a subject that is not as productive for them, as opposed to something else that would be much more productive and useful. Although the deep oceans of the world may be fascinating for you to learn, unless you are actually going to be a diver, it may not be the most productive thing for you to learn. Another example may be if you are interested in computer hacking, although that may be appealing to learn, you can get into an incredible amount of trouble if you were to apply computer hacking in your life. The point is, that you should be focusing on learning things that you can apply in your life to help you get from where you are now to where you want to go in the future. There is so much focus wasted on things that we perceive as being of high value, but in reality, it is of little use to us. When you learn to eliminate things that are not helping you to grow, you will become an achieving machine.

Another binary that will help you to achieve is to recognize temporary from permanent. Is what is happening in your life permanent? Or is the thing that is happening temporary? To learn something is temporary and to know something is permanent. Pain will always be the subject of temporary and pleasure will always be the subject of permanent. People complain a lot about things that are temporary and will soon be gone. In the greater scheme of life, everything is temporary, but an extended period of time is deemed as permanent. Are you writing your goals in pen, something that is permanent? Or are you writing your goals in pencil, something that is temporary? When you write your goals in pen, they will never go away, even long after you achieved that goal. When you write your goals in pencil, you can temporarily read your text until you decide to erase the pencil writing.

I encourage you to write your goals and dreams in pen so that you can see it clear as day. Too many people are writing in pencil and there are eraser bits everywhere because they do not follow through with their goals and their dreams. Always write in pen because pen is not going away and pen is darker than pencil. When something is darker, it becomes a lot more real than when something is lighter. When you write your dreams in that dark pen, it automatically becomes more real. When you can rewire your brain and realize that the temporary is not permanent and the permanent is not temporary, it will give you the confidence to surrender your excuses, doubts, and procrastination.

This next binary is probably going to be the most controversial subject in my entire book, but it is important. You may not agree with this one, but it proves effective. Am I going to be truthful? Or am I going to lie? The truth is great, because the truth never changes, but sometimes you need to lie. This is because we do not live in a perfect world. If everything in life were honest, what would be the point? If everything in life were dishonest, what would be the point? Life evolves through truths and lies. Everybody in this world lies and is lied to. You have to see reality as it is. Your parents will lie, your teachers will lie, your employers will lie, your employees will lie, the government will lie, the news will lie, sales people will lie, your client and customers will lie, professionals will lie, your children will lie, and even you will lie.

Everyone lies, especially in the market place. If honesty were in every commercial, the whole market system would collapse. Would you really buy a product if the advertiser told you how bad the product was? There are countless reasons why a lie may need to be told. The idea here is to lie strategically. Faking it until you make it is necessary sometimes, but how you go about it is important. If you are going to lie, make sure that you are not hurting anybody. Too many people are taken advantage of way too easily because they are very kind and honest. It does not make you a morally bad person to lie as we are conditioned to believe. You have to calculate the size of your lie effectively, because if the lie is too big, it will be exposed or it may not be exposed. If the lie is too big however, it has a much greater chance of being exposed. Lies can be used in the greatest ways possible because lies are binary.

You must make calculated good lies because good lies create good outcomes and bad lies create bad outcomes. Realness can be converted into fakeness and fakeness can be converted into real- ness. Something was faked until it was made real and something real turned into fakeness. To live as honestly as you possibly can is the best, but since life is not perfect and people lie to you, you may need to lie in some cases. Lies can be beautiful because it is a creation of the human mind. Too little lies can be bad and too many lies can be bad. Too little truth can be bad and too much truth can be bad. Live honestly and bend the truth purposefully. Lies are good or bad and everything is best in Balance.

Something that a lot of people do not consciously realize is that there is a difference between knowing and believing. There are a lot of people that know things that they just do not believe in. Do you know about it? Or do you know about it and believe it? There is so much to know out there and there is a lot of knowledge that people tell us and we take their word for it. You may know about what is happening, but you may not really believe it. You may know that people in third world countries generally have harsh living conditions, but you will not believe that knowledge unless you actually go and visit a third world country with these conditions. When you see something, experience something, or something opens your mind due to the environmental stimulation, you will know and believe it. You may know that the essence of business is to create something of value and to sell it, but unless you have produced a product of value and sold it, you will not truly know and believe it. You have to live something to know about it and believe it. You may think that you do not like chocolate ice cream, but if all you have ever had was vanilla ice cream, how would you know that you do not like chocolate? If you tried chocolate ice cream, then you can make your decision and know and believe it. The theme here is that unless you have done something, you really do not know about something.

Are you living in fear? Or are you not living in fear? Most people are living in fear and feel deep down that they are incompetent. People are primarily scared of what others will think of them. Challenge your core beliefs if you are living in fear. People fear because they think that they have to get something perfect. The truth is, by actively engaging and by working, it is a lot better than telling yourself that you cannot do something. Write a list on a piece of paper with one column that says, "Why I think I can" and another column that says, "Why I think I cannot". You will quickly realize that if you can put one reason why you can do something, that means that you can 100% do something. The only hard part that you need to tolerate is the emotional fear when you are trying to complete a goal. Remember that like any pain, emotional pain is not permanent and it will pass. You are strong enough to silence the emotional pain and head in the direction of your goal. The only thing that fear roots from is emotional pain. Every kind of pain, no matter what way, shape, or form, will always subside.

If you only realized that your brain is powerful beyond measure and that people heavily underestimate the power of their brain. Everything that has been created in the world has been created because of someone's brain. Music is made by the brain, business is made by the brain, art is made by the brain, emotion is made by the brain, technology is made by the brain, dreams are made by the brain, goals are made by the brain, rules are made by the brain, buildings are made by the brain, advanced math is created by the brain, imagination is created by the brain. Knowing this, it is ridiculous to believe that your brain is not capable. Everyone has a brain and they are essentially similar. You just need to maximize your thoughts and actions with your brain how your brain was designed. Your brain can do anything that it thinks about. If your brain can think, "I can build a house" you are 100% able to build a house if you put in the time to learn.

Perhaps this story about my grandfather may inspire you. A long time ago, my grandfather bought some property and decided to build a house on it. At the age of 22, he decided that he would build a house all by himself. He hired somebody with a backhoe to dig a hole for his house. After the hole was dug, he did not know what to do next and he sat in the bottom of the hole and began to cry. When the neighbor saw that my grandfather was crying, he asked him, "What is wrong?" My grandfather said, "I do not know what to do next!" The neighbor told my grandfather that he would help him build the house. If you can believe it, after some time, my grandfather and the neighbor built the entire house from the ground up. With electricity, plumbing, and all of the works of a standard house.

After my grandfather built the house with the neighbor, he eventually began to build multiple houses all by himself. Every house that he owned, he built the house himself. The point of this story is that my grandfather could have easily cried in the hole and gave up, but he was determined to put his mind to building a house and worked incredibly hard to reach success. Too many people today dig a hole, cry and complain about how it is impossible, and they never make another attempt to build a house ever again. This just goes to show, if you can think it, you can do it. The only thing that it will require is dedication, focus, and hard work. There is simply no substitution for putting in the work. The only person that can put in the work is you.

You need fear to have the courage to go after your goals. You need to act in the face of fear to shine and to realize your greatest dreams. Getting over the emotional fear and achieving your desired goal is the majority of what gives your goal a sense of value. If you did not get over the emotional fear, you would not appreciate your achievements as much as you would if there was no fear to get over in the first place. There are two people in this world. The people who act in the face of fear and the people who do not act in the face of fear. If you can master yourself and your environment, there is nothing to fear, because the world starts to become comfortable. When you start achieving, it will boost your confidence and things you feared in the past will not even scare you. Fear is always going to subside once you have certainty in your mind that you were able to reach the end goal. The more that you achieve in the face of fear, the more that the fear will eventually go away.

Are you seeking help? Or are you not seeking help? Humans are naturally very stubborn and think that they know everything. Nobody can do everything by themselves. There is not one big business that was ever created by one person. A team built every great business. It may have been one person that created the initial vision of the company, but there are always more people involved with the growth of the business. How can your business grow without the help of paying customers? The better the team, the better and more likely that the business will scale largely. Nobody is adept at every possible skill. Everybody has their strengths and everybody has their weaknesses. You may want to reach out to someone that is better at that something than you. It is always better to do something from a place of strength, not weakness. When you have the humbleness to go to someone that is more knowledgeable, more skilled, or more experienced, you will learn something. Since no two people have the exact same life and everyone lives a completely unique life, we all have different approaches to things.

This is helpful because that means that you are able to learn from a broad range of people. One person may help you learn in one way and another person may help you learn something in another way. The best people to learn from are people that have a higher proven skill than you. Believe it or not, some people that possess a greater skill than you may just be waiting for you to come along and ask them for help. The reason for this is because most successful people want to see others achieve success. The person may also relate to your situation that they were once in when they needed help to learn. Unfortunately, not every successful person is nice, but it only takes one or a couple of people with a higher skill set than you to help you grow and to learn the skills for yourself. Do not be afraid to genuinely ask someone for their help. You may be surprised to see how helpful people can be, because humans are naturally loving and want to help. If you do not take the time to seek out help every now and again, you may find yourself not pro-gressing as fast as you would like to be. Everyone is going to need help at one time or another. If humans were designed not to seek help in this life, there would not be any other human beings around.

If you can even donate $10 every week to your local homeless shelter or any cause that you feel is worthy, you will achieve a sense of fulfillment and karma will come back to you. Karma is very real. Karma is also known as a form of the law of attraction. Karma and the law of attraction repeatedly prove to be existing in this world and the more good that you do for others, the more likely it is for that success that you have helped others achieve to come back to you in some sort of way. It is hard to feel bad for yourself when you are donating money or your time to something that you believe in, even if it helps just one person. People complain that they do not have money, but you will always have time to give. There are simply no excuses. If you complain about money and you are not giving out money or time, how do you expect the world to allow you to receive?

There are many people struggling in the world, more than one person can help. But if you can make a difference in even one person's life, you are doing what it is to be a loving human. We were designed to be loving creatures, but the environment that we have been exposed to has caused us to be filled with hatred and to neglect love. You are always going to be the product of your environment. Whether or not you are the product of your choosing or of unconscious conditioning depends solely on what you expose yourself to. When you create love, act in love, and put love into your surrounding environment, the world has no choice but to multiply that love and bring that goodness back to you. The more people that you are helping, the more love and goodness that you are spreading. There is not one single person out there that has ever achieved a great amount of success without having a philanthropic compassion for humanitarianism. If you think that even $1 will not make a difference to a cause weekly, you are heavily mistaken. However you can help, do it.

You cannot help anyone unless you first help yourself, but one of the best ways to help yourself first is to add value and success to other people around you. If you think that there are not any immediate problems that you can help out in the world, go downtown to any city that you live in and it will open up your eyes. You will never succeed in this life if you do not help others to succeed. You can promote the success of others if you can just reach deep down into your soul with great conviction and to give all of your gifts and talents that you have been given to the world.

This binary is one that is life changing and will alter your mind for the better. If you apply, it will completely transform your life. This binary is called osmosis. Are you practicing through osmosis? Or are you not practicing through osmosis? Osmosis is learning something by improving your understanding and retention of something. It stimulates your mind by helping you make connections of two things. The reason you need to learn about osmosis is because learning is passive. Humans actively learn. We may not even be trying to learn and yet our minds allow us to learn.

To give you an example, say that you want to learn music. You can choose to learn any genre of music through osmosis. How does this work? Simply listen. If you want to be a guitarist, listen to the guitar and the accompanying instruments. Hear what the guitar is doing. Listen to the genre of music over and over and over and over again. Keep listening until you can internalize that sound inside of your mind so much that the internalized music in your mind becomes instinctual for you to play on the selected instrument. Of course you will have to practice the physical instrument to produce the sounds of the instrument, but when you can internalize the instrument's sounds with the selected genre's sound, you will be able to instinctually play.

This does not only apply to music. Part of the magic with practicing osmosis is that it can be applied to any element of your life. You may want to become a master of business. You will need to remember that you are always going to be the product of your environment. Only through osmosis of your physical environment, you are going to acquire skills. To learn business, you need to expose yourself to a business environment and internalize all the business jargon based on the genre of what business that you are into. When you feel the setting, feel the conversation, and feel all of the stimulations associated with being in a business environment, you will naturally begin to understand it. You will not instantly understand the dynamics of business, but it will come to you after the process of exposing yourself to the business environment over and over and over and over again.

The more that you expose yourself to your desired learning environment through continuous repetition, it will force your brain to internalize the environment so that the new knowledge will remain inside of your mind. After an extended period of time, you will instinctually be able to perform the necessary actions to convey your internal interpretation of a subject. Constantly expose yourself to the environment that you want to learn and your mind will eventually emulate what it is being exposed to. The emulation of the mind causes your body to move according to the mind's interpretation of the environment through osmosis. Keep doing until you become. Expose your mind until your mind becomes.

The question is if everything in life is binary. The answer to that is yes. Everything is completely binary because it is on either one extreme side or the other extreme side. Everything is either a 0 or it is a 1. Every decision that you make in the course of your life is going to be the result of one decision, or the other. It is going to be Black and White. You are either going to be on one side or the other side. It is a simple approach to decision making and it is completely necessary for you to calculate which side you are on and which side is the best side for you to be on. Although everything in this universe is binary, this is just the basic knowledge that you need to know. Now that you have the basic knowledge, we are going to be getting into a lot more depth. You are going to be learning how to transfer light source into darkness and everything in between that will create the proper Balance.

The biggest thing that I want you to get out of this chapter is to write on a piece of paper all of the reasons why you think that you can do something and on a second piece of paper write down all of the reasons why you think that you cannot do something. Write down on the second piece of paper every last doubt and reason why you think that you will fail. Next, I want you to take that second piece of paper stating all of the reasons that you think that you cannot do something and then crumple that piece of paper up and throw it into a recycling bin. Be on the binary side that believes in yourself and acknowledges that you can do something about your situation. You can improve the quality of your life if you decide to be on the correct binary side. The correct binary side is the side that allows you to empower yourself, and to take action in your life. You need to take action to get to the place where your goals, desires, dreams, purpose, and fulfillment lie. It all lies within you to live the greatest life and you can have it if you choose the correct binary. It does not matter what decision you make in life, you just need the better binary. There is always the good binary and the bad binary.

Absorb this content over and over again and you will think very differently. You have to expose yourself to the right environment and there are countless environments for you to expose yourself to. Good environments and bad environments. The two habits that you can master are mastering good habits or mastering bad habits. You have decisions to make in life based on your past decisions. You will have present day decisions and you will have future decisions. Be careful when you make your decisions because your decisions may influence for better or for worse your future decisions that you will have to make.

Apply binary in your life. Take action and confidently head towards the place of your greatest happiness. Sometimes you do not need a reason to be happy. Nobody cares about you more than you ever will. Do you.

2

Balance

In the last chapter, you learned that everything is binary and that you are either on one end or on the other end. This is great knowledge to have and it will serve you well in your decision-making. Life being life, it never has only one answer, because the binary of mono (one) is poly (many). Although thinking in binary is going to help you substantially in your decision-making, it should only be used as the basis for your decision-making. You see, this book was named Black and White Balance because there is always the middle. The middle is what Balances the two ends and holds them together. You have one side, the other side, and the middle. The middle is not as simple as you think it is. It is not just 0 middle 1, it goes to a much greater extent than that. The scale from 0 to 1 is called a spectrum.

You are going to learn about how spectrums can help you with your decision-making. If you were patient enough to have read the first chapter, then you are patient enough to read and understand this concept, as each chapter builds on the last chapter. When you have the final product and all the concepts fit together in your mind, your brain will alter. When your brain is altered, then you can make better decisions and create new outcomes in your life. When you finally alter your mind, you will learn that taking action is how you are going to change your life.

Time to learn how spectrum will change the way that you think. Much like 0 and 1, a spectrum looks like this:

0. 1

The 0 and 1 is the binary of our decision. As you already know, you choose to be on one side or the other. Are you living in the future? Or are you living in the past? Now what if I asked you if you are living in the far past? Are you living in the present past? Are you living in the future past? Are you living in the past present? Are you living in the current present? Are you living in the future present? Are you living in the past future? Are you living in the current future? Are you living in the far future?

As you can see, there are lots of things that can be put into the middle of Balance. This is very important to grasp, because it will allow you to see all of your options in decision-making.

Everything in this universe can be classified and put on a spectrum of some sort.

Fashion is a spectrum:

Outed . . . . Modern

Above are the two binaries of fashion but you have everything in between to Balance the two ends. Types of fashion that can be in between outdated and modern could be vintage, bohemian, chic, artsy, sexy, casual, formal, sophisticated, tomboy, rocker, preppy, flamboyant, exotic, vibrant, elegant, athletic, hippie, business, teddy boy, greaser, punk, cultural, classic, luxury, designer, street, country and countless other styles of fashion.

Sexuality is a spectrum:

Homosex . . . . Heterosexual

There is LGBTQ (lesbian, gay, bisexual, transgender, questioning) and there is heterosexual. My personal position is on the heterosexual side of the scale. No matter where you are on the scale, I find it completely beautiful to express yourself as what you are. It is always better for two people to make love and be happy around each other, regardless of their sexuality, than to have hatred. Humans are humans. If people are happy and not hurting anyone, then there is absolutely nothing wrong with what they are doing. Let people be happy. The sexuality spectrum between homosexuality and heterosexuality is bisexual, pansexual, asexual, questioning, bi-curious, gray-a, androgynous and many more. Some people may be sexual, non-sexual, or in between sexual and non-sexual. You can never just have the two binaries. Love is love and sexuality is important to understand because there are much more than just two identities. When you learn about sexuality, you will learn that even non-human beings have same sex sexual relations with each other. Sexuality has been around for a very long time and has always existed in many forms.

Light is a spectrum:

Darks . . . . Lightness

You can be in a room that is pitch dark inside. In the exact same room, the light can be bright. The same room may be very dark with just a dim light glowing. The same room could be bright with a faint darkness. The same room may be equal in darkness and lightness. Any place that you go to has the potential to be any shade between the two sides. Every single color has lightness or darkness. You can have a light purple room, or you can have a dark purple room. The same applies to any color. As you move closer to one of the binary sides, it will alter the shades of brightness or darkness.

Money is a spectrum:

Money . . . . Money

Money is on both sides because it is such a large spectrum to talk about. The spectrum money to money could be all of the currencies out there, from US Dollar to Yen. From liabilities to assets, from negative interest to positive interest, from inflation to deflation, from high stocks to low stocks, from appreciation to depreciation, from short-term investment to long-term investment, there are countless spectrums associated with money.

Politics is a spectrum:

Left . . . . Right

Some of the most common political structures include communist, socialist, green, liberal, democratic, conservative, progressive, libertarian, anarchy, republican, and fascism.

Emotion is a spectrum:

Sad . . . . Happiness

Emotion in between happy to sad range from loathing, rage, grief, ecstasy, admiration, terror, remorse, awe, love, optimism, joy, annoyed, surprise, trust, jealousy, hatred, anxiety, depression, calm, bitterness, and anticipation. There are simple emotions and there are complex emotions. Simple emotions may require less energy. Complex emotions may require more energy.

Music is a spectrum:

Minor . . . . Major

In music, there are three families. The families are major, minor, and dominant. There are four qualities that a chord may be. Major chords, minor chords, augmented chords (extreme major), diminished chords (extreme minor). There are so many variances in major tonality and minor tonality. There are no wrong notes in music. There is only varying level degrees of suitability and deviation in notes. Some notes work well with others and some simply do not. There is fast music, slow music, happy music, sad music, simple music, complex music, and several various genres, with all come from a wide range of cultures. Everything in music fits perfectly into any musical spectrum that you map out between the two binaries. You can create your own binaries and spectrums on any subject.

Health is a spectrum:

Unhealthy . . . . Healthy

What you consider to be healthy and what the next person to you considers as healthy is going to be different. Everyone has a different interpretation of what it means to be healthy. Health is a very broad subject that has so many elements to it, such as sleep, diet, exercise, stress, and other variables. You can see how health would be a spectrum based on the topic and individual needs. To keep it general, you could be unhealthy, healthy, less than healthy, not healthy, but not unhealthy, almost completely unhealthy, binary healthy, binary unhealthy. Like in any scale, we could say that you are completely on one side of the binary or completely binary on the other side. That is why in this example you could be binary healthy or binary unhealthy. Spectrums are potentially limitless.

By now you have had plenty of examples of how things are always going to have more than just two sides. This opens your possibilities to a whole new world of possibilities. Sometimes you just need to determine the Balance that stabilizes the two binaries. Ask yourself if there are binaries within the two binaries that you are looking at. Ask yourself if there is another spectrum that you have not thought about yet which would counterbalance this spectrum.

0. 1

Original Spectrum 1

1. 0

Counterbalance Spectrum 2

As you can see, sometimes you will need a counterbalance scale to Balance the initial scale. To acquire the counterbalance scale, it may require some creativity to give meaning and to figure out your interpretation of what is missing

Counterbalance Spectrum 2 is the binary spectrum to Original Spectrum 1. When you have created your Counterbalance Spectrum 2, it will give you more decision-making options to formulate a better decision.

The real reason that you should be thinking in spectrum compared to just binary is because it offers more potential solutions. In life, you are going to find yourself on spectrums. You are always going to be on a spectrum, whether it is a relationship spectrum, financial spectrum, work spectrum, time spectrum, emotional spectrum, health spectrum, fashion spectrum, business spectrum, spiritual spectrum, sexual spectrum, nature spectrum and many other spectrums. The key here is to ask yourself where you are on the scale and determine where you want to be on the scale.

Once you have determined where it is that you want to be, it is up to you to take the necessary actions to change your position on the scale. When you are able to figure out how easy it is to recognize where you are on the scale and that you can reposition, you will be growing at a very rapid pace into your newer and more evolved happier life. The adjustment might be very subtle and small. The change might be easier than you thought it would be. However, sometimes the repositioning that you are undergoing on the scale may take longer than you anticipated.

This all goes back to the basic virtue that you must master: patience. There is absolutely no escaping patience. It may take some time to reposition yourself where you would like to end up on the scale. If your repositioning takes longer than anticipated, do not give up. If you give up and do not deploy patience, you will remain on the exact same coordinates as you were in the first place. When you are able to become patient and to move slowly towards the side of the scale or binary that you would like to go, you will get there. Sometimes, you can jump to reposition yourself on the scale. Other times, you simply need to put in a lot of effort, have a lot of patience, and work towards the new position on the scale. Sooner or later, you will get there. It is a matter of mastering the scales of life. Scales of life are surrounding us everyday and at every moment. New scales are created daily. Life is very multidimensional.

When you are able to think in terms of scales, you can think in a much more multi-dimensional way. If you look at an object in 2-D, you may miss some of the 3-D elements that make all the difference. You can consider binary as 2-D and your thinking in width or area. You can consider a scale as 3-D because then you are thinking in much more depth and volume. This scale is a system and you need to implement systems that work in your life. Some things work better than others and you need to find out what works best for you. When you have a system, it is your foundation for you to consistently make sense of things and your surrounding world. When you understand your world and environment, then you can know yourself.

Sometimes what you are looking for is right in front of you.
Sometimes what you are looking for is beside you.
Sometimes what you are looking for is behind you.
Sometimes what you are looking for is not so obvious.
Sometimes what you are looking for is not even there or anywhere.
Sometimes you need to worker harder.
Sometimes you need to work smarter.
Sometimes you need to work hard in a smart way.
Sometimes you need to work smart in a harder way.

In some very rare circumstances you may not even need to work hard or smart at all. You may be in the right place at the right time.

You may be in the right place at the wrong time.
You may be in the wrong place at the wrong time.
You may be in the wrong place at the right time.
You may be in the right place at the wrong time and at the wrong place at the right time simultaneously.

You may be in the wrong place at the wrong time and nothing
  bad happens.
You may be in the right place at the right time and nothing good
  happens.
Maybe nothing at all happens. Maybe no action was taken.

A mistake might bring you massive success. A mistake may bring
you horrible misfortune. Success may bring you tremendous failure and disappointment. Success may bring you fulfillment and
joy. Imagine all of the lottery winners that lost all of their fortune.

You might be the same in the future. You might change in the
future. You might change now and still be the same in the future.
You might change now and be different in the future. Imagine a
new wardrobe, same person.

Maybe we have full control of our life. Maybe we have no control of our life. Maybe life happens to us instead of for us. Maybe
life happens for us instead of to us. Maybe we are not real. Maybe
we are real. Maybe life is real. Maybe life is not real.

Everything can be questioned and put on a scale. Every scale
can be filled with information, so always keep an open mind when
writing scales. You may just think of the greatest innovative thing
in existence from writing a scale of things that have already been
created and done. You can fill all of the empty parts of the infinitive
scale with ideas that have not been created yet. When you write
a scale and explore your possibilities, you may find that there are
unlimited opportunities. Whatever you believe in and whatever
you do not believe in can be questioned and mapped out. Give
yourself the best position on the scale that you desire.

Your dreams are on a scale:

Your Night. . . . . Your Dreams

You may be living in your worst nightmare because you are not
allowing yourself to move to the more desirable binary or a better

46

position on the scale. It all starts with you in your personal life, taking action in order to move on the abstract idea of the scale. You need to take real actions to move on the abstract scale.

Somebody may like you.
Somebody may not like you.
Somebody may really like you.
Somebody may really not like you.
Somebody may have the potential to like you.
Somebody may have the potential to not like you.
Somebody may not like you but they may also like you too.
Somebody may like you for good reasons and not like you for bad reasons.
Somebody may like you for bad reasons and not like you for good reasons.
Somebody may like you because you have something that they want.
Somebody may not like you because you have something that they want.

There is endless amount of pinpointing that you can do on a spectrum if you get creative enough and keep on thinking what else you may add to your scale.

You may be on the scale.
You may be off the scale.
You may be on and off the scale.
You may be more on one side of the scale.
You may be more on the other side of the scale.
You may be right in the middle of the scale.
You may be on several different parts of the scale
It may be impossible to be on several different parts of the scale.
It may be possible to be on several different parts of the scale.
Maybe there are not several different parts on the scale.
Maybe there are several different parts on the scale.

You can go back and fourth by yourself, countering everything that you are saying. This skill alone can help you get in touch with your creative side. When you are unsure what to do, ask yourself. The brain is immensely powerful. You have a brain, a mind, and a soul, which should all be working together in harmony to get you through anything. The body is a complicated thing and people do not know the power of themselves. You only have one space suit in this life and people abuse it to the extreme. However, in your space suit you have the brain.

The brain was designed for thinking and you can work out your brain by allowing it to think. Your brain will start to grow when you use it. I challenge you to think of something that you want to resolve or complete in your life. Once you have that thing in mind, ask yourself why have you not achieved it yet? If your answer to that is an excuse, change your answer. If it is an excuse, ask yourself why is this reason in the way? Ask yourself how you are going to deal with it. I will give you a further example.

Your statement could be, "I want to raise $100,000 in venture capital."

If this were my question, I would ask first, "Who do I know who has $100,000?"

If I did not know anybody with $100,000, I would then ask, "If not who, then what business may have $100,000?" There are shows that give investments, there are people who are investors, there are people that know investors. You need to get creative and ask yourself the right questions until you come up with right answers.

Become solution based. Become a problem solver. The problem many people face is that they focus too much on the problem and they do not focus on what they should be focusing on: the solution. When you focus on coming up with a solution, your problem will go away. How are you going to make things better if you are focusing on the problem? It will never go away. Get down and dirty and think of how the problem could be solved, solve it, and then the problem will go away. When you think enough about a solution, sooner or later you will inevitably come up with a solution if you want it bad enough. If you focus on the problem, no matter how bad you want it to go away, it never will.

This scale that I am going to give you will be one of the most effective tools that you will ever have to fight off problems in life. Ready?

Problem . . . . Solution

Beautiful scale! If you are on the problem end of the scale, you can ask yourself question after question after question after question until you come up with a solution. You should not doubt yourself. You can do this. You can solve anything if you are resourceful. You can generate a sound solution. Maybe not all by yourself, as you may decide that you need certain people or a business to help you. Believe that if you ask yourself a question, you can answer it.

"How am I going to get out of debt?"

"Why am I in debt?"

"Because I have been spending too much money on things I do not need."

"Do I still have the things I do not need?"

"Yes"

"Why not sell the things that you do not need to help increase your wealth?"

Just like that, you are already formulating solutions and you are being much more calculated in your decision-making. Whatever your problem is or may be. You can ask yourself anything. Nobody thinks to have conversations with themselves. We as a society deem that as being crazy. Nobody is telling you to talk to yourself aloud in a public place, but you can sit at a desk quietly and write down your thoughts. Write your question down on a piece of paper and answer that question, then answer that question, then answer that question. Keep going until you come up with a solution.

I believe so much in this practice that I use it for every major problem in my life. Sooner than later, I come up with solutions using scales exactly like the ones in this chapter. You can create any scale. Have conversations with yourself. The solution to any problem that you may face in life is deep within yourself and you have the access to reach it if you dig deep enough. In any case in life, if you dig deep enough, you will eventually hit a precious resource such as a diamond, gold, or something else of tremendous value. The same is true with digging deep in yourself through questions of your mind to yourself.

It is so easy to complain about being poor and to say that you want more money. Change that thought and focus on the solution, which is being richer.

It is so easy to complain about being heavy or unhealthy. Change that thought and focus on the solution, which is getting to your ideal body type and being healthy.

It is so easy to complain about being in a bad relationship. Change that thought and focus on the solution, which is deciding what a happy relationship looks like to you.

It is so easy to complain about having a bad job that you do not enjoy. Change that thought and focus on the solution, which is finding the things that make you happy.

It is so easy to complain about how you are losing at something. Change that thought and focus on the solution, which is how you win.

It is so easy to be jealous of a person's talent, skill, or gift. Change that thought and focus on the solution, which is figuring out what they did to get there.

It is so easy to talk your self out of completing your goals and dreams. Change that thought and focus on the solution, which is discovering how to make your dream come true.

It is so easy to obsess over what could go wrong that you end up doing nothing. Change that thought and focus on the solution, which is to occupy yourself only with the things that could go right.

Too many people in business focus way too much on their product. The quality of a product is essentially irrelevant if you have high quality marketing. Do not focus on the product, because you may be focusing on the wrong thing. Keep in mind though, a bad product will eventually hurt you in the end. The scale that you could apply would be what you should be focusing on and what you should not be focusing on. When you become solution based, everything becomes possible.

People try to become experts and sometimes becoming an expert is not the point. Of course, you are going to want to achieve mastery, because then you can add much more significant value to the world. Mastery is only achieved by putting in the time. To do what you love and to monetize your mastery is essential. Everyone is capable of mastery.

However, sometimes acquiring enough skills to solve a problem is good enough. If you learn enough to solve a problem, you have done your part. People tend to get carried away and want to know a lot about something before solving their immediate problem. It all goes back to what you should be focusing on and what you should not be focusing on. There is a hierarchy of priorities for you to learn.

Probem . . . . Solution

With this scale, you can bounce from problem to solution quickly. It is not the scale that is going to do the work, but how you use the scale is what is going to aid you in helping yourself. When you can pin point from where you are on the scale to where you would ideally like to be on the scale, you can reposition to the desired place. It only takes minor creativity and a little bit of work and you can do anything. No matter what you do in life, you have to have a scale and a system. This book creates principles for you to apply to your life. You are smart enough to create your own system in life. This is going to sound crazy, but you do not even need this book to succeed. When you are able to find a system that works for you, apply it, and enjoy the benefits of your system.

Failure is a result of lack of creativity. People constantly procrastinate and are lazy. You may have to look yourself in the mirror and admit to yourself that you are lazy. The greatest gift that you can give to yourself is honesty. When you are honest with yourself, that is your opportunity for change. You need to think deep down within to find what could potentially work for you. Get creative. There is a system that works for each one of us within and it is for you to find that system. Laziness prevents us from being resourceful and creative. When you learn to be resourceful and creative, you can have anything that you want.

If you are able to comprehend and accept this concept, your life will change. That concept is for you to get up early, put yourself in a position to succeed, work hard, be patient, be creative, do something differently, and enjoy the success. People lie to themselves and tell themselves that success is easier said than done. That is just a story. Mathematically, it makes sense that if you work hard and you sacrifice enough, you will achieve your desired result. If you do not work hard enough, think hard enough, be patient hard enough, and work smart hard enough, you will not succeed. Do the thing that helps you get to that next quality of your life.

You can do it, do not just read "success" books and attend seminars. You have to be all in or all out. Do not tell people what you are going to do, just do it. I know that I am being a little aggressive right now, but I only want you to win. The truth may hurt, but the truth is the only thing that is going to help you. You need to just do. Go for it, you know what it is that you need to do in order to succeed. There is no such thing as taking a step in the wrong direction or any other cliché sayings. When you take one step in front of the other, you will be in a different place. Have faith that things are going to work out if you just keep walking.

Here is a concept for you:

You CAN'T . . . . .You CAN

You see, there are two binaries above. One says, "You can't" the other binary says, "You can."

False . . . . Truth
One side will always be true and the other side will always be false. Now one cool thing that you can do with scales is to realize that you can apply the truth or false scale by overlapping any scale that you choose.

You CAN'T . . . . You CAN

False . . . . Truth

Just like that you can see clearly that "You can't" is always going to be false and that "You can" is always going to be the truth. Every time that you look at "You can't" it is always going to be false. Every time that you look at "You can" it is always going to be the truth. One binary is always going to be wrong and the other binary is always going to be right. You can give binaries meaning or you can give them no meaning. You can give your story a meaning or you can give your story no meaning. You tell yourself stories about why you can do something and you also tell yourself stories about why you cannot do something. It is your life and you give meaning to binaries. You can give your binaries meaning or unmeaning. You can cancel anything out. You make the rules of your life and how you want things to go. If you want it, you can have it. Never ever give up and keep going until you are there. The biggest reason that people fail in life is because they give up too soon.

They fail because they give up too soon.
They fail because they do not believe in themselves.
They fail because they are not consistent.
They fail because they lack the discipline.
They fail because they are scared to go against and do something different.

They fail because they do not plan.

They fail because they are scared of failing.

They fail because they want too much too quickly.

They fail because they lack the proper humility.

They fail because they create excuses.

They fail because they do not network with the right people properly.

They fail because they do not take advice.

They fail because they do not learn from past mistakes.

They fail because they let distractions take over.

They fail because they procrastinate.

They fail because they do not accept responsibility for their decisions.

They fail because they lack creativity.

They fail because they lack confidence.

They fail because they talk themselves into failing.

They fail because they expose themselves to failing environments.

There is a countless amount of reasons why people can fail and are going to fail, but there is no such thing as being fail proof. All you can do is keep showing up and working hard until you succeed. The only way to succeed is to fail. The greater your failure rate that you have, the greater that your success rate will be. You will become successful when you get rid of fear and manage your emotional state when fear arises. In fact, the thing that we fear most is the best thing for us.

Failure is the best. If you were always succeeding, what would be the point? If you are always succeeding, you are not living. If you can embrace failure and understand that for every failure that you have, you are one step closer to your inevitable success. When you pour everything into something and you fail, it will give your success so much more meaning. You would not value your success if you did not fail before achieving success. The more times that you achieve failure, the more valuable the success will be. It is a mathematical equation that is always true. Big creates big and small creates small. Generally because small may create big and big may create small. From a general point of view, the more you put out, the more that you will receive. It is within your reach if you believe it. It is also out of your reach if you believe it too. For better measure, focus on that it is within your reach and that you are going to have it. Rewire your brain and appreciate your failures in life. Failures are nothing more than a stepping-stone to your successes in life. To never fail is to never succeed.

Like I said in the beginning, I do not like to talk about myself a lot, but there was a time when I never thought in a million years that I could write a book. The idea scared me, but you are currently reading my book because I was able to put in the time. Every day, I set aside time to write and to generate ideas. I would lie down on the bed and think about nothing until something clicks. I realized that my best ideas are formed when I am in a place where there are no sounds to distract the flow of my thoughts. Naturally when writing this book I would think, "Would the reader like what I have to say?" "Would the reader not like what I have to say?" My response to myself would be that it did not matter rather the reader liked what I had to say or not. The only thing that I kept in mind is that I am writing from a place of love and I will add meaning and goodness to someone else's life. When you do something from a place of love, everything becomes a lot easier because it becomes authentic, caring, and sincere. I had no idea how my book was going to look, how it was going to be written, how it was going to be published, or anything else. All I knew was that I was going to write a book, and I believed it.

Even starting a book with no ideas was terrifying, but when you just keep thinking, and believe that you have some goodness to share, anything is possible. There are always doubts about what other people, including my family, may think about the book. It simply does not matter, what matters is writing a couple of pages a day and having faith that the book will one day be complete. What also mattered was putting in the time to write the book and saying "no" to people. Eventually, the book was able to be complete and put into the hands of many readers to inspire them to live out all of their dreams.

Like myself writing this book, you can live out your dreams by working hard and dedicating the time. You will see that if you consistently put in the time and get a little better than you were the day before, you will eventually get there. Your mission in life is to wake up and be better than you were before you went to bed. If you want to start something or are just starting, you can do it. If it scares you, the fear will subside if you just start doing it and living it.

When you keep doing something, the results will always be revealed as you get better. When you get better, your results get better. You can live your dreams and become great at something if you just start doing it. Actively work towards that dream and it will come true. Like I wrote one page at a time until this book became complete, you are going to write the pages of your life. It all starts with writing a couple of pages a day, after some time, you will have a book. Keep learning, keep growing, and keep working on ways for you to develop yourself. Get out there and live a different life. If all you do is what you have done before, you will receive the same as what you have done before. If you change and do something differently, you will have a new outcome presenting itself to you. It really is that easy, the only hard part is getting over yourself. You are the greatest ally to yourself, and you can also potentially be your worst enemy. It is for you to focus on being the greatest thing to yourself. The only thing that is ever stopping you from your dreams and your goals is you.

If you want a better business that is busier, then you have to get busier. Nobody knows or cares about your business unless you go to them. Knock on doors if you have to. Your life will not change until you change yourself. If you want to get rich, then you have to get richer. If you want to become more successful, then you have to get more successful. We become what we are. We are what we do consistently without fail. To produce great, you need to study great. Constantly concentrate on anything that you do until you master it.

There is no such thing as luck. Humans use the word luck as an excuse for why things happen and why things do not happen.

Everything is destiny, and you can control how your destiny will unfold to a greater extent than you may think. If you created your whole destiny, what would be the point? However, you can certainly shape your destiny by your decisions into your most approximate ideal destiny. Things happen the way that things happen. Being born poor is not being unlucky, because if everybody was born rich, what would be the point? Different life experiences create different learning experiences. Even the person that won the lottery is not lucky. They found themselves in a position that could help them succeed. The same is true with you. Put yourself in a favorable position that could help you to succeed in something. If someone is truly great, they are not lucky. If someone is truly great, they put in the work. A hiccup of life is not lucky or unlucky, it happened by destiny.

People may argue that there is luck to some extent, but there is no such thing. If something did not happen to you, it is because it was not meant to happen to you. If something happened to you, it is because it was meant to happen to you. Life is in constant struggle between the forces of bad and good while trying to create a Balance. Everything happens for a reason because if it happened for no reason, what would be the point?

In love, people think that there is only one soul mate. That may be true, and that also may not be true.

One Soul Mate. . . . . Multiple Soul Mates

You see, people come into our lives to teach us something. How could one person teach you everything? Also, how could multiple people love us the exact same way?

That creates another spectrum.

Like . . . . Love

There is a level of how much a person can love us. It can be differentiated and vary greatly. If one soul mate comes into your life at the right time, they may love you a lot. Another soul mate that comes into your life at the right time may love you a little. You may love a soul mate a lot, or another soul mate a little. You should have the mindset that you are able to love many people throughout the course of your life. However, everyone has such a unique life and you may only have one soul mate in your life. It is consistently inconsistent and inconsistently consistent.

In life while learning, you will never learn everything. Learning is limitless. You can be knowledgeable and live a life with much wisdom though. When you think you know the question, the answer changes. When you know the answer, the question may change. Things are always changing. Changing things may be constant and constant things may be changing. What appears may not be and what may not be may appear. Balance the binaries, and the binaries will be Balanced. Live out your dreams and your dreams will be lived out. Believe in yourself and you will be believed. Live without fear and fear will not be lived. Keep doing until something meaningful until you have done something meaningful. Put in your hard work and time and time will show your hard work. Live evil and evil will have lived. Learn to teach and teach to learn. Give love to receive love. It is easy to live and to live is easy. You do not need education to go to school and you do not need school to have an education.

Lot of backwards talk helps you to understand things better. If it is forward, it can go back. If it is up, it can go down. It can also be Balanced. Your brain is so capable of making sense of the world and taking action to recognize your greatest dreams and goals if you just use it. People have brain capacity that they do not use.

When you look within the middle between the two binaries for other answers and solutions that you can apply to your life, that is Balance. When you identify your position on the scale and then reposition your current position on the scale to your desired position on the scale that is Balance. Lastly, when you are stuck in the middle between the two binaries, look outwards toward the ends of the scale and you will find your Balance.

3

Silence

In the last chapter, you learned that everything could be mapped out using scales and spectrums. You also learned about the tremendous power and capability of your brain.

The truth is that we live in such a noisy and fast culture where people do not feel that they have the time to grow or do productive things, so Tony Yip become complacent. Things move way too quickly and people are consumed with way too many thoughts, which is not healthy. No human should have so many thoughts that they become stressed out and paralyzed. Thoughts are great and can be very beautiful, but sometimes you need to just stop, calm your mind, and feel the presence of silence to recuperate your mind, body, and soul. You need to learn to empty your mind, because when you do, you create the ability to have new thoughts come into your consciousness.

It only takes one great thought to come into your mind to change your whole world. Something happens to you when you put yourself in a place where you are at total tranquility. Your physiology changes and you become a lot more peaceful. Silencing the mind is the single best thing that you can do for yourself. Think of what it is that you want to achieve, think of where you are in your current life, and think about where you want to go. Remember that it is okay to slow down your mind to find yourself. People get so lost in the noise and how quickly everything happens. Have a release of thought. Close your eyes and feel the silence and get in touch with nature. No matter what it is that you are going through, when your eyes are closed, and the environment is silent, things are always going to be better. Keep your mind as relaxed as if you were sitting on a couch in a far away place looking at the ocean.

You can heal your whole life when you have silence to be alone and to work through your thoughts. The quality of your thoughts will become a lot better. People have been meditating for thousands of years and it is something that every human being needs in their life. Slow down your thoughts and keep calm. Distractions occur because your environment is too loud, too fast, and too interesting. Human beings are not robots and we need to recharge our batteries. When your mind is working, your battery is draining. When your mind is calm, your battery is charging. The brain is what controls everything in your life.

Have you ever noticed that when you go into nature, it is mostly silent? Why is that? Because silence is an element of healing and nature's purpose is to heal. Nature grows plants and beings and it also heals wounds. The power of silence is going to heal your mind and quality of life. There is a reason that the human mind is prone to headaches when things are too loud. Humans rarely get headaches when things are silent. Silence is a sound and the sound is silence. At any funeral that you have attended, silence is present to honor the life of a person. When there is no one talking, and no noise is present, silence sustains. Silence is a very powerful force. When you listen to someone, you can only listen by being silent. When we are dead, everything remains silent for eternity. When we learn things from a young age, we learn in silence before we create noise. Listening to silence is going back to the basics.

Everything in this existence is based on silence. Our heart rhythm beats in silence and we cannot hear it beat through our chest without a device to amplify the sound. We think in silence. Money grows and is spent in silence. Everything that produces noise eventually becomes silent. Work, school, friends, family, music, streets, offices, malls, stores, everywhere that you go to is consumed with an incredible amount of noise. The noise stimulates your mind and requires you to hyper think. Your thoughts perpetuate at such a rapid rate that your thoughts do not slow down, but speed up. You need to withdraw yourself from sounds every now and again.

When you are in a silent environment, you can focus on your breathing, your thoughts, your creativity, and what is important to you. Silence is about taking recognition of what is important to you in your life. Sounds consume and suffocate our life so much that we mentally strain ourselves, which increases our levels of irritation and decreases our ability to remain calm. Silence will always be the most beautiful sound that you will ever hear in the course of your life and it will never be unenjoyable to listen to nothing. When we become calm because of silence, our life becomes calm. A calm life is always a happier life.

Take a moment to think of all the noise and thought pollution that you hear on a regular basis in your environments. You can feel all of the angst that is building up in your mind from the continued exposure to all the sounds. Life is too fast. People are always behind schedule because we allow ourselves to take on more than we are capable of handling. Going faster can actually cause you to be going slower and going slower can actually cause you to be going faster. When you recharge your mind with silence, you can speed up your thought processes and that will help you to become more accomplished and to live the next higher quality of your life.

You see the power of silence all the time without even realizing it. The people that say that they are going to do everything end up doing nothing. The people that say nothing are usually the ones that end up doing everything. Like the saying goes, you should not tell, but show. Showing is always silence and telling is always noise. Silently work and work silently. Do not say, but do.

You cannot learn anything if you are speaking in a conversation. You can learn everything by listening in a conversation. In a conversation, being optimistic and listening to what someone has to say is silence. When you judge, remain close-minded, and do not allow yourself to try and understand what someone is saying, you are letting noise get in the way. When the noise of your close-mindedness gets in the way, it will hurt you and hinder yourself to experience potential growth.

In communication, there are times where it is healthy and effective to have silence. If there were no pauses created in communication, it would destroy the dynamics of the conversation. Life is all about building tension and releasing tension. When you are speaking, you are creating tension. When you pause, you release the tension. Sometimes no words at all are more powerful than saying anything. Learn to communicate and create silence at the right time to be a more effective communicator. If there are no silent moments in a communication, there is just noise. Patience and silence are the two virtues that will enhance the quality of your life and they must be learned. You cannot be helped and grow if you are not able to listen and be silent.

When you create excuses, procrastinate, doubt yourself, and have fear, that is just noise. Silence is positive and noise is negative. Silence your excuses, silence your procrastination, silence your self-doubt, and silence your fear. Silence everything in your life that does not serve you. Have silent serenity and get rid of noisy negativity. Silence the noise. Silence the negativity in your life. The first thing people do when something goes wrong is panic. People should silence the panic and allow themselves to enter a state of calmness and tranquility.

When you go to sleep at night, you experience silence. There is a time and place to make noise and that is when you need to stand up for something, someone, or yourself. You need your dreams to go from silence to reality. There are times that you will need to address things and promote your business. Noise is in great abundance. Before noise, there needs to be silence first. The world and universe was created in silence before there was noise. Silence helps everything.

Your mind needs silence, your spirit needs silence, and every aspect of your life needs to have silence. Trees grow in silence and they are always silent until the wind pushes against their leaves.

When the leaves are being pushed, it is still very quiet. The ocean is silent, but you hear quiet waves. The night is silent. The soil in the ground is silent. Become one with silence. Listen. I am a firm believer that we were given two ears and one mouth. The two ears were created to listen more than we speak with our one mouth. We were designed to listen to noise and to silence. Noise knows nothing without an element of silence. To say something can mean nothing and to say nothing can mean everything. Actions will always speak louder than words. Take action in your life to better your life. Words are just noise until you silence it with action. You are the one to take action and silence the noise in your life. You cannot be heard until something is silent and you cannot hear until you are silent.

We live in a digital age and social media is the way of the world. It is life changing and will help you in business. However, media is full of noise. Pictures are silent, but can mean many words. Those words from the picture are noise. The more pictures and articles, the more noise that you are exposing yourself to. You need to take social media breaks and filter the information out of your system. Social media is a primary platform of excessive noise that may hurt you if you expose yourself too much to it. Your cell phone ringing all the time and having to talk to people daily is noise. Take breaks from your cell phone and the Internet to recharge. News feeds are full of noise and sometimes that noise needs to be silenced. Being connected to silence in reality is much deeper than silence on social media. Social media is a silent activity, but if you take breaks from social media and connect to silence in the offline world, you will find a much higher state of calmness and relaxation.

Approximately 90% of all communication is non-verbal and no matter where you go in the world, you do not even need to speak the same language as the people around you. You could go anywhere in the world, point at something that you would like to purchase, and give currency without ever having to say anything to the merchant. Currency is silent, yet it can talk. Something that is beyond wonderful in this world is how people with no hearing can communicate. People without any hearing can communicate through their sign language where they only use their body to communicate and not one word is spoken. Some of the most talented people that have ever lived were unable to hear. What these people are unable to hear, their mind may make up for it in some other extraordinary way. People that are unable to hear and live in complete silence are some of the most spiritual and calm people that you will ever meet. Less is more sometimes and fewer words can say a lot more than more words do. The greater silence from the less words can create a tremendous impact.

Take a look at any piece of art and you will create your own interpretation. You will feel overwhelmed with emotion and awe. Everything in life is art including every profession. Once you learn the art of something, it only becomes easier. Art may make you laugh or cry, make you happy or sad. What you were looking at was just a painting, yet it said so much even though it did not say one word or make one sound. Art speaks to us in such a profound way in complete silence.

In any movie that you may watch, the most mysterious silent character is almost always the most captivating character. When someone is mysterious, they are almost always quiet. In romance, mystery is highly seductive. Mystery is silence. If mystery were noisy, it would not possess its mystique and allure. Humans naturally romanticize the unknown in life. That is why it scares so many people to take action in their life and go towards their dreams. Our dreams are silently mysterious because they are unknown and unlived. Just like romance, people are so fearful to approach the unknown that they miss out on the opportunity for the greatest thing to ever happen to them. Imagine having said something to someone rather than just letting the moment pass. Learn to love the silence and the unknown. When you are living your dream, it will no longer be silent. Your dream is only silent until you achieve it. Humans are scared of silence and of loneliness. If you can just learn to love the silence, embrace the silence, and experience pleasure from silence, your life will become different. To love silence, you need to practice being around silence. Go away temporarily from the noise and the fast paced society that we live in and come back refreshed. It will be the best thing that you have ever done for yourself. Focus on the stillness to clear your mind.

The past is noisy because we have lived in the past and we have heard it. The present is the noisiest time because we are living in the noise. The future is always silent and still, but the silence will become noisy. The greatest thing is that you can find silence in the noisiest time, which is the current present that you live in. We can apply silence to a binary.

Silence . . . . Noise

You can ask yourself what binary each environment in your life is. Adjust your position on the scale from one environment to the other to become closer to your ideal binary. One environment may be completely silent and the other environment may be completely noisy. Some environments are a mixture of silence and noise. Some environments are more noisy than silent and some environments are more silent than noisy. Ideally, for the greatest euphoria and calmness, you will want to find an environment in your life that is completely silent. Find the type of silence that is completely still to have the greatest recharge.

Stare at a blank piece of paper, it is still. The blank paper is silent. If you draw, write something, or make a mark on it, it creates noise. If you write down your dream in silence and can see your dream that you wrote down, something magical happens. The most special thing in the world happens and that is your dream creates a noise. When you silently write your dream on a silent piece of paper, that dream and piece of paper creates noise. When you write down your dream or draw out your dream on a piece of paper, you are one step closer to making that dream a reality. You are one step closer to taking action to realize your dream in reality. If you think your dream is impossible, go to a silent place. When you are at the silent place, take out your silent piece of paper and make it noisy.

When the noise is loud enough, the universe will hear it. It is then up to you to make that noise known to the universe. In silence though, you have to believe that it will come true and that it will work. Get rid of the noise that tells you that you can't. You can! You can achieve anything that your heart desires if you just silence the noise. You can, you will, and nothing will stop you. Fail in the noise and you will succeed in silence. Fail in silence and you will succeed in the noise. Silence is the greatest recipe for success.

The silent treatment is incredibly powerful and it gets to everybody. The reason for this is because silence is incredibly loud. If you have ever been ignored intentionally, you will know that pain. Being ignored is the most hurtful thing in the world because it is rejection. Rejection is silence. People are so scared to fail and then be ignored by other people. That is the essence of fear, the fear that people will disregard you. If you are truly great and you work hard, and you embrace the silence, you will be too great and too powerful to be ignored. Silence will transcend into noise, and noise will descend into silence. Silence the fear that you are going to be ignored if you fail. If you never fail, you will never succeed. The greatest saying is that the master has failed more times than the student has tried. Failure is just noise. Work hard in silence and then you will silently succeed.

If you are in a cave, or a large empty room, it is silent. If you say something in the silence, it will echo and come back to you. For whatever you say in silence, it will echo back to you in reality. Every time without failure, but the echo needs to be fulfilled first. Only you can take action to make the echo in your life. When you understand the echo, you will achieve the greatest level of fulfillment and joy in your life. Go get paintings, writing, or anything that is silent and still. Put them up in your place or room. When you feel overwhelmed, look at the art or text and feel the essence of silence and peace. Feel like you are a silent body of water. Very still, and any ripples that you create will only multiply silently.

A single smile is silent, yet it brings so much joy to people. It even makes the person that is smiling in silence feel happier. Allow silence to heal yourself. Every breath that we take and every second that goes by, we are silently dying. Every moment we are silently approaching death. It is important to live your life to the fullest and make the best of your life. Do not be so quick to think or to speak. Think in silence about what you want to do before you do or say anything. Slow down your breathing and take a deep breath in silence, it is harder to concentrate on your breathing in the noise.

Noise increases our levels of adrenaline in our brain and adrenaline causes stress. Over time, that stress will grow. Humans are not designed to take on a high level of continued stress. Humans are meant to be creatures of peace and calmness. When you have more silence throughout the day, it will promote less stress. When you have less stress before you go to bed, it will give you a better quality of sleep. When the quality of your sleep is high quality, you will perform better. When your levels of noise are high and your brain takes in a lot of stress, it will be harder to have a higher quality of sleep. Over time, this will weaken your energy levels and happiness.

Something you already know is that it is much easier to focus on something in silence. It is much more difficult to complete something when your surrounding environment is filled with noise pollution. This alone proves the power of silence. It is hard to feel overwhelmed when silence is around you. Silence is caring and silence will never pressure you. Silencing the mind will be your greatest challenge in life if you want to heal. With a little practice, you will be able to embrace silence. If you say something that you do not need to say, you are only creating noise.

Silence is powerful because it helps us to reflect on our life, our actions, our thoughts, and this reflection will help you learn about yourself. Silence gets other people to put their attention on you. Silence allows you to feel empathy for someone else. When somebody says something unintelligent to you, silence can be the best answer. Silence is a question and silence is an answer. Silence is able to speak when words cannot say what is needed to be said and silence can let someone know that they did something wrong.

There is always a reason to speak, but you do not need a reason for silence. The most silent person is often the person that is the best to listen to carefully. Silence can be a source of strength because it is so easy to create impulsive noise that may not help us, but actually worsen things. Work hard in silence and let your success make the noise. To be silent is to create silence. Get rid of the noise and silence will arise. There is magic in listening to nothing, you will feel something.

To prove how powerful silence is, the next page has not a single word on it. It is completely blank and silent. Focus on the blankness of the page. Look right in the middle of the page closely and do not look anywhere else. When you look at the blank page, silence your mind. Avoid any of your thoughts that come. Take this exercise seriously and really believe in the power of silence. When you look at the blank page, you will feel the presence of silence. You can take that same silence and experience it in an environment in your life.

After you look at the blank page, close your eyes. Think of nothing and focus on the darkness of your inner eyelids. Remove all thoughts that enter your mind. Think of blankness, think of calmness, and think of peace. Then open your eyes and look at the blank page again. The page is silent until you put words or markings on it. When you make even a single dot on the page, you give the blank page noise. Feel nothing and allow your mind and soul to recharge. Get yourself out of the noisy world that we live in temporarily and feel the comfort of silence.

Focus on the crisp blank page and feel calm. Make sure that you are away from any noise around you. Take this book somewhere quiet and be ready to look at the page. Silence is a superpower. It is one superpower that will help you understand things in life. Why things are the way that they are. The creator of the universe is the most powerful thing in the universe because the creator is always completely silent. Look at the next page and feel the power of silence.

Feels relaxing, doesn't it? The page had nothing on it, yet the silence gave it so much meaning. Your level of calmness has been heightened and now you can embrace the positivity and empowering thoughts into your mind gracefully. You have removed all of the noise that was once in your mind. When you are in this state, anything becomes possible. If you are experiencing hardship and difficulty in life, remember that the pain is temporary and temporary is the pain. The things that are temporary are never permanent and the things that are permanent are never temporary. Always fall back on silence through difficult times and to maintain the good times. Whenever things go wrong and you feel unpleasant emotions, look at a blank page. The silence of the blank page will cure your pain.

To feel silence, remove all communication and things that you hear. Feel the spiritual connection of silence. When you feel the absence of sound, a deeper connection is reached. If you watch silent films, not only are they incredibly entertaining, but they will inspire relaxation into your life. In music, rests are known as silence in a piece of music. When there is a rest in music, it gives the listener a chance to reflect on the previous sound that was played. Rests in music creates dynamic for the music. Music is a conversation with comfortable moments of silence. Someone that is playing may play something, then pause, play something else, then pause.

Silence can help you in every aspect of your life. If you work for somebody, listening to your boss in full detail may help you understand what they may want. If you know what your boss wants, you can go above and beyond what their wishes are. By doing this, you will become more valuable to the company. When you become more valuable to the company, your income will go up and your position in the company will also improve. Listen up and then you will go up. If you are an employer, listening to what your employees have to say about the company, customers, or any of their duties will potentially give you better insight on the company as a whole. This is important to know because then you may be able to come up with a better system that will promote greater success of the company. When you find the root of why your customers, employees, or supervisors are upset, you can change everything around more favorably for the company. When your managers, employees, or other people of the company are happier, they will work harder and your company will increase profits because the customers are satisfied.

Being a business owner means taking into account what the needs of your customers are. The only way that you can determine what the needs of your customers are is to listen. Listen in silence to every word. The greatest teachers in any business are your customers. Customers will directly or indirectly indicate why they will not do business with you. You just need to listen to your customers. People want to be heard and understood. When people feel loved, cared for, and understood, you will have influence over them because you have opened them up. The only way that you are going to have a clear vision into the hearts of people is if you are open-minded and silently listen to people's needs. In business, when you are kind and people feel that you care, they are highly likely to give you their business. It all stems from you silently listening to them. Silently listen to the market place and current events in the world because it will help you greatly in business.

In relationships, people always argue because they do not take into account compromising and understanding what their partner's needs are. If you are in an argument, it is because you are not listening to the needs of your partner. When you silently listen to the needs of your partner, you can grow the relationship. If the relationship is not growing, it is dying. The only way that you are going to grow the relationship is to listen to the needs and to understand your partner. Breakups happen when people do not listen to each other and they start to become distant and grow apart. People run away from arguments, but if you can just selflessly put your feelings aside and really consider what the person that you love is trying to get you to understand, everything will change for the better

In finance, if you do not listen to how much you are spending and how much you are saving, you will not have money. You need to listen to your bank account. Your bank account is a reflection of how well you understand your finances. If you ignore the numbers and you do not take the time to do the math and to calculate your financial decisions, then you are not listening. Your bank account is the most silent thing in the world, yet it will create the most noise for your life if you are not careful. You and your money are in a financial relationship. When you learn about money and finance, you are caring more about your financial relationship with your money. When you care about your financial relationship with your money, your money will start to care for you. When your money cares for you, life potentially can become more calm and easier. Money is a taboo subject in this society, but money is highly important in life. Financial stability generally helps to create a stable mind. Try to have a stable mind anyway. Financial stability enhances your stable mind. You need to get your finances in order. Have a good financial relationship by listening to the numbers. Money is a relationship of numbers.

In health, if you are becoming very overweight and sick, it is because your body is giving you the signs and you are not listening to it. Your health is in a relationship with you. Everything is in a relationship with you and you need to listen silently in every relationship. Life is a relationship and if you do not listen to your life, your life may end. If you are exercising, eating right, and studying healthy ways to live, you are having a good relationship with your health and your body will thank you for it. If you neglect giving your body the fuel and energy that it needs to function, your body will let you know that you are neglecting it. The noise will be a growling stomach. When the stomach is fed properly, it will remain silent. In anything that you do, all you have to do is to listen in silence.

Your happiness is in a relationship with you. You need to listen to your happiness. Your happiness is a much easier relationship to have than you may think. Do what makes you happy. If you are doing what makes you unhappy and you are not changing the things that are making you unhappy, your relationship with being happy will suffer. Evaluate if something is making you happy and understand what makes people feel happy. Happiness generally stems from doing things that you love and doing the things that bring joy to you. If you are unhappy, you need to silently change that unhappiness to happiness. Your happiness relationship will be noisy because you will know if something is making you happy or unhappy. Silently think of a solution to change the status of your unhappiness to happiness.

To learn to be silent is to have self-control. Silence is better than lashing out emotionally to something. Silence will give you a chance to calculate before attempting a new challenge. Silence will give you the chance to think before you speak. Silence is a powerful substance that will bring you much wisdom in your life. Silence is a weapon that can be used for good or for bad. Use silence for good. When you use silence for good, it has a much stronger impact.

You need silence to reset your mind. Go find your inner silence.

4

Confidence

The truth is, we live in a very insecure and broken society. Humans are exposed to things that are damaging to their confidence. There is plastic surgery from cosmetic surgery to any form of beauty surgery that you could possibly think of in order to alter the body to promote aesthetic beauty. It is something that not only women do, but men do too. People may take artificial drugs to change their physical appearance. Men may take steroids to increase muscle mass. People dye their hair, apply make up, and get tattooing such as micro blading. There are technologies and apps that digitally alter a photograph of a person's appearance. There is a lot of artificial beauty in the world, especially in advertisement. There is nothing wrong with altering your appearance if you need specific work done or if it makes you feel good about yourself.

The reason why so many people, especially teens, are insecure is because they compare themselves to online photographs. There is no way that the viewer could naturally look the same way that some of the photos portray and it picks away at people's confidence. Some pictures can completely destroy someone's confidence. People mistake altered beauty as being natural beauty when it is simply untrue. Some of the most secure people in life have something that can completely destroy them and overwhelm them with insecurity. We live in a time where people that seem the most confident are the ones that are the most insecure. Not only is it pictures that we see, but it is also what we are told about ourselves. Marketing is a lucrative business because it exploits your insecurities and fears to emotionally influence you to buy a product from a brand. When people are emotional, that is when they make decisions. It is a lot easier to manipulate a person when they feel bad.

We live in a culture where sex is such a high priority and the frequent subject of conversation. When people feel that they are not worthy to reproduce because they feel ugly, they may purchase things in order to attempt at increasing their sexual market value. We may feel incapable of being loved because we do not look a certain way, feel a certain way, or live a certain way. These are all just stories that we tell ourselves. We glorify things that do not mean anything. Do not let anything damage your confidence.

The youth glorify drugs and think it is cool to take party drugs. Peer pressure affects many teens and young people. Some of the music is responsible for promoting the glorification of drugs. They think that cocaine is a status drug and that rock stars and other big time people do it. The idea that drugs are cool gets into the minds of so many people and ruins their lives. They think that it is cool and that nothing will happen to them when they consume drugs. It is devastating to see the youth giving into peer pressure and taking high levels of prescription drugs in order to achieve a high. Especially in the youth, when their brains and bodies are developing, that is when they should not be consuming drugs.

People romanticize financial status and social status. Many people, especially men, feel incredibly intimidated by other men with more money than them. People will go on social media sites and see people post pictures of large amounts of cash, which has an impact on their confidence if they are financially struggling. People become so insecure that they withdraw money just to post the cash on their social media sites. People rent exotic cars and make other people think that the high-end car belongs to the renter. People lease and rent things and other people may automatically think that the person owns the expensive item when they really do not. Money is the biggest source of insecurity in most people.

Everyone wants to have money and we may feel less worthy if we do not have it. Money and your level of success is something that should not define you or be the only root of your happiness. All you are doing is buying into the story (fantasy) instead of what something actually is (reality). You never know what somebody has and what somebody does not have. You should not be concerned about anyone else's perceived success whether it is real or portrayed to be real.

There are a lot of songs in popular culture that glorify high-end cars that most people could not afford. Again, it is a story being told to convince you that these cars are extraordinarily special and that you are someone important if you have one. In my personal life, I have had the privilege to drive someone's $500 car and I have also had the privilege to drive someone's $1,000,000 car. If you name it, I have probably taken it out for a drive. Guess what? They all have one thing in common. They get me from point A to point B. Lavish high-end cars are thrilling in the beginning, but like everything new, it eventually loses its novelty and the flame dims. I have had inexpensive belts and expensive belts, and they both held up my pants. I have been to prestigious gyms and community gyms, and both provided me with the same workout.

I have hung out with the wealthiest people, the poorest people, ordinary people, and extraordinary people. I was able to have fun and learn from every one of them. At the end of the day, we all put on pants the same way. We are all one, a brotherhood of humankind. Nobody is a God and no one is better than you, they just do things differently than you. You are capable of greatness, just like anyone else is capable of greatness.

There are pros and cons to everything in life. Like being famous may sound good on paper, but it may not necessarily be what you think it is. There are always pros to being famous and there are always cons to being famous. Becoming rich sounds great, but there are pros and cons to wealth. Just like driving a $500,000 Lamborghini. Although everybody and their dog may be staring at you while you step on the gas, it just gets you to point B. The cons of driving a Lamborghini are an increase of pressure on yourself because everyone is watching you drive it. You may have good attention from car enthusiasts, but you may also attract really bad attention. People may hate you for driving a car that they cannot afford. Although you should not care what people think, it just may not be the kind of attention that you want. You also have to worry about parking a high-end car. Curious people are going to be rubbing their nose up against the window and jealous people may smash a window or key the car. You are going to be constantly approached by people that do not care about you, but want to bother you about the car.

When I drove someone's Ferrari for the first time with the convertible down, at every red light people would say, "Nice car!" "How does it feel?" "How much does something like that go for?" "What do you do for work?" "Want to trade cars?" and countless other bizarre questions. People would ask question after question from point A to point B. It was cool in the beginning to enjoy all of the attention, but after driving the Ferrari enough, I started to get a little annoyed with the repetition of questions and attention from other road users. Everyone wants to take a picture of the car, they want to sit in the car, and they want to ride in the car. Many people glare and assume that you are a jerk.

Although high-end cars are fun and they look cool, there are a lot of cons associated with them. Not to mention it is uncomfortable to get in and out of high-end sports cars. At the end of the day, it is just a hunk of bolts and metal just like any other car on the road. Nothing special. It is best not to idolize anything in life. You should not put an extreme amount of importance on something that is most likely not as special as it is made out to be.

Confidence will save you. You need confidence in life. Everyone is going to have faults and insecurities. No one is perfect and no one will ever be perfect. No matter what you do in life, you need to approach something from a place of strength, not weakness. If you approach something from a weak and insecure place, you will fail. If you approach something from a place of confidence, you will succeed. The most effective thing to apply into your life is to learn how to shift from insecure to confidence. Use this binary.

Insecure . . . . Confidence

Ask yourself, am I confident about this? Or am I insecure about this? This is going to be a tough chapter for many people because it is hard to be honest about your insecurities and weaknesses. It is necessary though, if you want to evolve.

I want to tell you a beautiful story that happened in my life that will inspire you. A long time ago, I decided to go to White Rock, British Columbia, Canada as I live in Vancouver, BC. From Vancouver to White Rock is quite the distance, but I wanted to go because it is and will always be one of my happy places. I went there and it was a cold, foggy fall. There is something about White Rock pier that speaks to me from a spiritual place. It is a pier surrounded by a breath-taking view of a great body of water upon the beach. If you do not live in Canada or have never been to the pier in White Rock, you must go there before you die. It will grab you by your soul in the most graceful and delicate way possible.

I walked down the great hill of West Beach to the boardwalk parallel to the beach. Feeling the cold gentle wind flowing through my hair and watering my eyes, sucking the fresh air into my nose, it stimulated my entire body with freshness and calmness. I proceeded to approach the base of the pier, watching seagulls fly in the distance. The pier is a very long walk to the end. I walked and walked, observing all of the tourists taking pictures of nature's beauty. Hearing the sounds of my feet stepping on the boarded pier and hearing the sound of the seagulls. Stillness surrounded me. It was the most calm I have ever been. I eventually heard music very softly. It was the sound of vibrations that I could not quite make out, so I walked further and further up the pier and the music became clearer and clearer.

I recognized the sound of a delicate sounding acoustic guitar. I walked further to see the strangest man I have ever seen in my entire life. The man had crooked yellow teeth, stringy grey hair, with a long green and grey hippie knit sweater. He was holding a guitar and had a great big smile on his face. I saw his street performance license and an open guitar case with coins in it. CD's were for sale in front of him. He had spiritual nature background music to play his guitar over. It was the most peaceful and beautiful music that I have heard to this day. Every note that he played had a purpose and the music spoke to me. I stood there watching him in awe as he was playing his music. People would pull $20 bills out of their pockets and buy his CD's. He was an eccentric man and would say, "Thank you, now autograph time", volunteering his autograph with a black permanent marker on the cover of the CD case. He would talk to the crowd at the end of the pier to engage them while he was playing his guitar and he would continue to play. He talked to me about the sounds that he was producing. I stood there and watched him play for 15 minutes. Life wanted me to experience something and it was the most dramatic thing. Because of this thing, I know that everything in life happens for a reason and that there is no such thing as luck.

What happened was destiny. After the 15 minutes of me standing there, rain instantly started to pour from the sky. He put his guitar in the case and the crowd started to evacuate from the end of the pier and headed back to the boardwalk. He then introduced himself to me. I was nervous, but I felt very comfortable around this man because he had a certain glow to him. He had a very welcoming and peaceful nature that drew me to him. He told me his name in his French accent and said that he was from Quebec, Canada. He was so intriguing to me and so enthusiastic about everything that he said with a great big smile. We walked and talked along the whole pier back to the boardwalk and we came to the base of the pier. I looked up and he asked me if I wanted to get some coffee at the restaurant that was right across the street. I agreed to get coffee and we walked across the street. The beach restaurant was closing because everyone was leaving the beach thanks to the fateful rainfall. We did not have any more time than 20 minutes or so to finish our coffee and go. There was absolutely no one in the dark restaurant so we sat on the patio that was covered from the rain outside. The waitress brought us coffee and went back into the kitchen. Absolutely not a soul was anywhere to be seen inside or outside. I felt that it was only he and myself in our own world in that moment. We sat there in silence after we put the sugar cubes in our coffee. Darkness surrounded, but he was the brightest thing in my vision, he had that glow. He said, "What is your favorite music to listen to?" I instantly and enthusiastically replied, "ROCKABILLY" which is 1950's style rock and roll (think Elvis Presley). He was impressed that I answered so quickly. His big smile lit up the table. He then asked me a question that completely froze my entire world.

He asked me, "What is your purpose in life?" To which I was completely lost for words. I was so upset that I did not have an answer for him. He then said, "If anything could happen and there was no way that you could fail, what would you want to happen?" I told him that I did not know. He then said to me, "I want you to have the same certainty in your answer about your purpose as when I asked you about your favorite music." He paid for the bill, walked me out, shook my hand, and he said that it was nice to meet me. He turned with his guitar case and I watched him walk away into the distance until I could not see him anymore. No cars were around and not a soul was in sight. I felt like life wanted me to live in my own world at that moment. I was stunned. I turned back slowly and proceeded to walk back up the hill.

I did not see anyone the whole way back and I sat and had a meltdown. I completely bawled my eyes and I felt defeated. Every insecurity in my life rose to the surface and any confidence that I had completely shattered. It was the most defeated moment of my life. Tears were running so fast down my cold cheeks and hitting the grass as it got colder. I was so alone in that moment. I did not know what I was going to do. I said to myself, "What is my purpose?" "Why am I here?" "Why don't I know my purpose?"

I felt lost and paralyzed with sadness. I felt like the whole world stopped spinning and life was not being lived by anyone.

I took a long time to get home that day. I arrived home late at night. Burnt out from all of my stinging tears running down my face. I did not have a single tear left to cry. I did not sleep that night. I thought that life was just a big freak accident that happened to me. I thought that maybe I would never find my purpose. Maybe I did not have a purpose. It was a hard year and I kept away from all of my family and friends. I always smiled even though I knew my heart was aching. Then something else happened by fate exactly 1 year later.

I met a doorman in Downtown Vancouver. He was a big, charming, witty man. He had the best speaking voice ever. I told him jokingly that he should be a commentator for sports. Then he told me about the events that he does aside of being a doorman. We talked for a while as I was working at a party that he was the doorman for. When our shift ended, I walked him to his car and his car was not there. Then we realized that there was a sign that said "No Parking". Things happen in life and I drove him in my car to the impound lot. At the time, I was so impressed by his mannerism in paying the fine to the guy behind the glass. We walked onto the lot and I asked, "How were you so calm about paying for the ticket?" He said, "There is no reason for me to get mad at him, he is just doing his job and I was in the wrong." It was absolutely incredible how he took action and responsibility for his life.

He then invited me to his house from for dinner. I was a little skeptical, but there was something about him that was calming and comforting. It was 10:00pm and we were still in Vancouver. I asked him, "Where do you live?" If you can believe, he said, "White Rock, near the pier." It was hard to believe that those words came out of his mouth because of my first spiritual encounter with the musician from Quebec exactly 1 year before. It was a long drive but I followed his car to his house, and sure enough, his house was right near the pier. I went into his house and saw his black cat. I was born on Halloween and I grew up with black cats and there is something about black cats that I am drawn to. I love the spiritual energy that black cats have.

The doorman cooked me a delicious bowl of spaghetti and it was very flavorful. He then offered me a strange looking dessert. I said, "No thanks" then he said, "Have you ever tried it?" I said "No" and he said "How do you know you are not going to like it if you have never tried it?" I slickly replied, "Intuition." He playfully said, "Just try it" with a big smile, as if he was implying that I was being stubborn. I said, "Alright" and then I tried it. It was the best tasting dessert that I have ever had and it was all his recipe and creation. He saw my smile and boastfully replied, "Not bad eh?" I laughed and said, "It was terrible" as I asked for seconds. He then said, "In life, you never know how something will be until you try."

After dessert, we went for a walk. I wanted to walk on the pier and he said, "Have you ever walked on East Beach?" I said, "No, always West Beach and on the pier." I said to him, "I do not know what is on East Beach." He said, "You will like it." I decided to trust him and we walked from West beach past the pier to East beach. It was breath-taking. I could not believe all of the restaurants and nature spot that were hidden away from me behind the bend between the two beaches.

As we walked on the boardwalk to East Beach, I became twinkly eyed because of the lights. It was such a sight. By this time, it was 1 in the morning. We walked so far down East Beach that we ended up under a bridge with train tracks above us. There was a very still body of water next to us under the bridge. It was a very peaceful sight. There were lights reflecting off of the water, even though it was completely dark out. Then a train came and it was very loud as we watched it go over the bridge. The train was honking the horn to let people in West Beach know that it was coming because there is a pedestrian train track crossing to get onto the pier.

The doorman and I stood there under the bridge still and I asked him, "What is the purpose of life?" He paused, and he said, "Too many people complicate their life, the purpose of life is to be happy." I was not expecting that answer at all. Years later, I realized that he was exactly right. We all have a purpose that is different and unique to our life, but the general purpose that we universally all share is that the purpose of life is to be happy. 2 years later, I realized my purpose for my life. The basis that every human shares is the purpose to be happy. What happiness means to you is your life's purpose. We overcomplicate our purpose. Our purpose in life is to be happy and that is it. Sometimes we do not need a reason to be happy. Sometimes true happiness and fulfillment is when we accept and are happy with ourselves. It is much better to simplify the complexity than it is to complicate the simplicity.

My life's purpose is to be happy. The thing that makes me feel the happiest is to help people realize within themselves that they are worth it, that they can live the life of their dreams, and live out their purpose. I was put on this planet to use my gift, which is my voice. My voice is something that I use to inspire others to create a better quality of life for themselves so that they can create a better quality of life for others. I realized that the only way that I am able to help people live their dreams and find their purpose is to make them realize it within themselves. It is my mission to make people's life the best that it can be because that is what makes me feel fulfilled. My fulfillment of helping people realize their gifts and talents gives me a tremendous amount of happiness and that is me living my purpose and dream.

I would never have known the beauty of East Beach unless I went. That is what I want you to understand. That you will never know unless you go. Just like how I went to East Beach. Go for it. Do what it is that you are good at and that you love. I know that it scares you, but if you look deep down, you can pull the strength out of yourself to complete your deepest desires and visions. You will fail, much more than a couple of times, but eventually if you keep going, there will come a day that you won't fail. You will succeed.

Since I first met the musician and doorman, I have never heard from them again. But I hope one day that our paths will cross again in the future. The way that I felt insecure about not knowing my purpose is the same way I learned if I want to have something, I could ask for it and it will come. You have to have faith and confidence that your answers will come to you if you ask for them and if you seek for them.

You need to practice confidence. The best advice I have for you to do is to go to that dark place. You need to ask yourself, "What makes me insecure?" Be completely honest with yourself. What makes you feel worthless? What are you weak at? What scares you? Once you have that insecurity in your mind, I want you to face it. You have to do this for yourself. I cannot help you do this. This is something that you have to do. When you face your insecurities and do the things that scare you, you will build your confidence.

If you are that shy person with social anxiety, I want you to say Hi to completely random people and try to have a meaningful conversation with them. Go to the mall, go to a park, anywhere where there are people, and just say Hi. You will be completely burned the first time. The second time, you will only be burned half as badly. As you get better at approaching people, it will only become easier. It will eventually become so easy that you will not even have to think about it. You will find that you will actually begin to like starting conversations. Through conversations with people, you will grow because you can learn something from anybody. Get out of your bubble. You cannot grow when you are comfortable. You can only evolve when you experience discomfort. The pain is temporary and temporary is the pain. When you stay comfortable, you will eventually become uncomfortable. When you are uncomfortable, you will eventually feel comfortable.

If you are scared of spiders, go find a spider and watch it. The longer that you watch it, the more comfortable that you will get. It will scare you in the beginning, but the fear will subside. Eventually that fear has no choice but to go away. Expose your self to what you fear and fear will leave. Everything is all in your head. Everything is in your head like the photographs that you see on social media. Most of the pictures that look nice may not even be close to that in real life. Change your story.

Here is the scale again for you.

Insecure . . . . Confidence

Go From Here . . . . To Here

Tell yourself it is easy and it will be easy. Tell yourself that it is hard and it will be hard. Change your thinking, change your story, and the outcome will change.

You are capable, you are strong, you are gifted, you are talented, you are beautiful, and you are loved. If you feel that you are ugly, I want you to know that you are beautiful to me and I am happy that you and I are on the same planet. I am truly grateful that you are sharing this world with me, even if we have never met in person. I want you to burst that bubble that you are stuck in and get out. Shine like the star that you are. Things can and will change. Trust yourself and learn to believe that anything is possible and possible is anything.

Like earlier in the book, you need to plant the bombs of your life. If you plant a bomb filled with confidence, that confidence will explode and scale largely. If you plant a bomb filled with insecurity, that insecurity will explode and scale largely. Everything in life is a downhill snowball effect. If you drop a snowball down a hill, it will only become bigger and bigger until it creates an avalanche. When you practice confidence and do the things that scare you, you are only creating a bigger confidence avalanche for yourself. When that confidence avalanche becomes bigger, you will trust yourself and believe in yourself much more greatly.

Another thing about confidence and insecurity is that people are scared to fail and remain insecure because they attach themselves too greatly to their success or failure. When you are attached to an outcome, you will suffer if it does not go the way that you want. Give up your attachment to success or failure and you will win no matter what the outcome may be. When you give up your worries you will lose your attachment. If everything went your way, what would be the point? You can make things go approximately the way that you want them to go if you are persistent enough.

You cannot be confident and insecure at the same time. You cannot fail and succeed at the same time. Only one thing happens at a time. You cannot live your purpose and worry at the same time. Excuses are fear's voice. When you are creating excuses, you are giving fear the chance to speak. When you give up your excuses, you do not let fear talk. In business, it is a complete waste of time for you to do something that you are bad at. Use the help of someone that is better than you are to accomplish something. If you do things that you are innately bad at, you will be working from a place of weakness, which sparks insecurity. When you are good at something, you will be working from a place of strength and confidence.

I bring this up frequently, but it is an important message in this book. The message is that there is no such thing as luck. There are no such things as accidents. Everything happens for a reason. You will feel confident if you are actively working on a goal and you will inevitably achieve that goal if you are putting in the work. You will feel insecurity if you are just hoping and wishing for something to happen when you are not putting in the work. Luck does not exist. The real truth is that you create your luck. You can and need to create your own luck.

To give you an example, say you really wanted to work for a company. No matter how badly that you want to work for the company, nobody is going to show up at your door. All of the luck in the world is not going to get you a position in the company. The reason for this is because luck does not exist. If you want the position in the company, you need to walk out the door and apply yourself. Nobody knows who you are until you show up. In fact, showing up is half the battle. If you go to the company that you want to work for, position yourself in front of someone that has the influence to make a decision in your favor. If you are able to show up, then you will get hired. Your chance of being hired by just staying home would be absolutely zero. The fact that you were able to show up and make an appearance is how you created your luck in getting hired.

If you admire someone and want them to mentor you, you will not receive any of their suggestions if you do not put yourself in a position to talk to them. The difference between the person that stays home and the person that goes to their mentor is that the person that went to the mentor is going to get mentored. The logical reason is because one person created their luck. The other person that stayed home and was hoping that luck would happen instead of them creating their own luck missed an opportunity. It is about acting on opportunity instead of hoping that opportunity will take care of itself. Things are not going to happen to you for no reason. If something did not have a reason behind it, what would be the point?

No one that has achieved greatness achieved it by accident. Through repetition and long hard work, the good becomes great. Good never becomes great by accident. Creating your own luck and practicing until you are great is the only way that you will recognize greatness. There is not a single person out there that you admire who did not create his or her own luck and greatness. Their greatness was created by their actions and dedication to something. If good became great without any work, what would be the point? If everyone were great without being good first, what would be the point? You create the outcomes of your reality. Not every outcome is going to be great, but every outcome will become greater over time. The harder that you work, the more luck you will create for yourself. Work hard. When you work harder, you create luck that makes things easier.

Say what you feel. If you keep something bottled up inside, you are only building insecurity. If you are able to openly express what you feel, you learn acceptance and you will become confident about what you feel. Too many people keep things inside and it kills them slowly. When you express what you feel to the world, you free yourself. When you free yourself, confidence rises. There is much pain in insecurity and much pleasure in confidence.

Humans were designed to be expressive and creative. If people did not express their thoughts, many of the greatest things in existence would not exist.

Talking through your problems will increase your level of reflection. When your reflection is thoughtful and vast, you will alter your creative mind and reflect on a potential solution to your problem. Reflection helps us become solution based for the future. When you find a solution to a problem, your confidence will grow. Although it is great to reflect, do not over reflect. When you over reflect, you complicate things more than they need to be. When you reflect the right amount, you are able to switch your mind from reflection of problem to solution of problem.

When you become confident and are confident, your belief in your ability to succeed will be heightened. Like anything, you are able to have too much confidence.

Confidence. . . . . Over Confidence

Too much confidence is not good because it may impair your sense of reality, which will cause obstacles. People may pay more attention to you, but the moment you fail because of your over confidence, people will make your failure known. People may challenge you because people tend to want to see you demonstrate matching your actions to your words. When you are confident and humble, you no longer become a target, and you will earn the respect of people around you. If people respect you, they may help your life in ways that you may not know. On the other side, having too little confidence will affect you as well. When you have too little confidence, it can prevent you from taking risks and action to completing opportunities that arise. If you miss the opportunities because of lack of confidence, it will hinder your potential to evolve. Have the right Balance of confidence.

If everyone were just confident, what would be the point? If everyone were insecure, what would be the point? Without insecurity, you could not learn to become confident. Insecurity is just an opportunity to create your confidence. Everything needs to be challenged from the other side of the spectrum to dance together. Every spectrum has a dance partner that Balances the other dance partner. Any insecurity that you could possibly have is capable of being overcome. Every obstacle in life can be completed as long as you start the obstacle and finish the obstacle. Never look too far ahead or too far behind, everything needs to be just the right amount.

Everything in this entire universe is calculated in numbers. One law of the world is mathematics. If something is unbalanced, it cannot be true. People lose confidence because they look too far ahead or too far behind. When you look just far ahead enough, you will be able to get to your end place. A car's light can only shine so far ahead. Never give yourself anxiety from not knowing and trying to push the spectrum's Balance too far out of Balance. No matter what obstacle that you approach, all you have to do is try and you will figure it out along the way. Have confidence. Like insecurity to confidence, defeat is the greatest secret to success.

This is your journey and you need to live it confidently. Living in fear and insecurity will create more things for you to be fearful and insecure about. Face fear and insecurity head on. When you are insecure and fearful, you create a world of depression for yourself. The depression spirals downward and it will keep you there if you let it. Depression can paralyze you to the point of not being able to get out of bed. When the insecurity breeds depression, you will allow yourself to tolerate abuse. When you are strong and confident in yourself, you will not accept anything that does not serve you and you will walk away from situations that are completely toxic in your life. Remember that confidence is a must but you need to be humble. When you are over confident, you allow yourself to learn nothing from your failures because your ego gets in the way. There is absolutely no way that you will succeed if you do not succeed in learning from your failures. If you achieve success and do not understand the meanings of your failures, then that means that you have failed to understand what true success is.

The best practice for you to transform yourself from a place of insecurity to security is to become more assertive and let what you want be known. When you put the energy out into the world about what you want, it listens. You must take the actions after you have said what you want.

The mathematical formula for success is:

Say what you want + Take the action = Success

If you do not do the math exactly in this way, you will fail every time. Mathematics is always a result of two or more. When something is just one, it is not mathematical and will not be Balanced. When you learn to be assertive in your life, you will have a strong fundamental core belief. It is a very powerful standpoint when you have your beliefs to fall back on. If you do not believe in something, it is easy to feel anxious. Imagine yourself when you were young. If your parents or guardians were not around when you were really young, you would feel uneasy. The minute the figure in your life came into sight with you, you would feel calm. The same is true with saying what you want and having confidence in your belief system. If your belief is strong and confident, it will be your parent belief that you will fall back on. Make your belief system strong and tell yourself that if you put in the work, you will get a little bit closer everyday to your destination point. If you have the confidence in your belief, you will trust that you will get to your destination in the future.

Belief is the most powerful key in execution. If you want to reach your goal, dreams, desires, happiness, fulfillment, then you are going to have to create your parent belief system in yourself.

"I am going to succeed"
"I am going to become wealthier"
"I will achieve my dream"
"I will change my life"
"I will become healthier"

"I will become stronger"
"I will not deal with abuse"
"I will not let my failures control my life"
"I will have happy relationships with people in my life"
"I will experience the greatest levels of love"
"I will become happier"
"I will recover"
"I am in control"
"I believe in myself"
"I see opportunity "
"I am committed"
"I am determined"
"I will not let procrastination, laziness, doubt, fear, or insecurity control me"
"I create my own reality"
"Life happens for me, not to me"
"I have abundance in my life and there is always going to be enough"
"Failure helps me grow"
"Starting before I am ready will work"
"If it were easy, everyone would do it"
"I will not let the past dedicate my future"
"I will not let an event be an end all be all for me"
"The future will be great"
"I will acquire the knowledge needed for me to live out my dreams"
"I will surround myself with positive and enriching environments"
"I will always find a way if I am determined"
"Everything happens for a reason"
"Little things bring me great joy"
"Everyday alive is a great day"
"There are no failures, only outcomes that help me learn to better myself"
"What I think matters and is important"
"I will only let empowering beliefs into my mind and not allow limiting beliefs"
"I can do something and can't does not exist"
"I will believe that I have it until I have it"

Every belief that enters your mind becomes your thoughts. Everything in your life is a consequence of the quality of your thoughts. You do not have to live your past and keep the same limiting beliefs in your mind. You can change any or all of your beliefs that you have about yourself, your environment, or the way things are. Have beliefs that are so powerful and so strong that they become your mountain that you can always look up to regardless of how things are.

If you take one thing out of this book, take this:

You control your beliefs, you can change your beliefs, your beliefs become your reality, and when you carry out your beliefs with the proper execution, you will only win.

You do not know how badly that I want you to have confidence in your beliefs and in yourself. I want confidence to rule your world and take you to that next place, the more evolved version of yourself. I want you to build a cocoon and evolve into a beautiful butterfly. Build your cocoon, build your confidence, become a butterfly, become confident in your life. Everything begins and ends with you, and only you. You create your beliefs and you change your beliefs. You live confidently and only you can live confidently in your life. You can change your whole life around when you shift even one of your beliefs to an empowering one that was once a limiting belief. It all starts with you and you can make the change.

When you change, "I can't be happy" to "I can and I will be happy" you will change your whole life around to match your new belief.

When you change, "I can't lose weight" to "I can and I will lose weight" you will change your whole life around to match your new belief.

When you change, "I can't earn more money" to "I can and I will earn more money" you will change your whole life around to match your new belief.

When you change, "I can't be accepted" to "I can and I will be accepted" you will change your whole life around to match your new belief.

When you change, "I can't be loved" to "I can and I will be loved" you will change your whole life around to match your new belief.

When you change, "I can't become healthier" to "I can and I will become healthier" you will change your whole life around to match your new belief.

When you change, "I can't live my dreams" to "I can and I will live my dreams" you will change your whole life around to match your new belief.

When you change, "I can't focus" to "I can and I will lose focus" you will change your whole life around to match your new belief.

When you change, "I can't succeed" to "I can and I will succeed" you will change your whole life around to match your new belief.

When you change, "I can't achieve greatness" to "I can and I will achieve greatness" you will change your whole life around to match your new belief.

When you change, "I can't believe in something" to "I can and I will believe in something" you will change your whole life around to match your new belief.

When you change, "I can't start a business" to "I can and I will start a business" you will change your whole life around to match your new belief.

When you change, "I can't afford it" to "I can and I will afford it" you will change your whole life around to match your new belief.

When you change, "I can't make the commitment" to "I can and I will make the commitment" you will change your whole life around to match your new belief.

When you change, "I can't help myself" to "I can and I will help myself" you will change your whole life around to match your new belief.

When you change, "I can't do what I love" to "I can and I will do what I love" you will change your whole life around to match your new belief.

When you change, "I can't learn confidence" to "I can and I will learn confidence" you will change your whole life around to match your new belief.

Everything in this entire universe starts and ends with you and only you. You have more power beyond measure that you do not even realize you have within yourself. To think that people in the graveyard do not have the opportunities that you have. You are so lucky to be alive and in existence. When you are dead, it won't matter. In 10,000 years from now, nobody is going to care about your failures, embarrassments, what you said or how you said it, and how well known you were or how unknown you were. Nobody will care because like you, they will be dead in the grave too. Disappeared from this world.

Knowing this, you should be inspired to take risks and to live your life. Say what you want to say, believe in what you want to believe, feel what you want to feel, and live like you want to live, because when you are dead, it won't matter. If you knew how lucky you are to live this journey on this majestic and awe inspiring planet, your confidence would be astronomical.

5

Time

Humans have developed the concept of time. There is really no such thing as time, there are only moments. Where you are now and where you want to be.

Time is measured in units...

A nanosecond is one billionth of a second (1/1,000,000,000)
A microsecond is one millionth of a second (1/1,000,000)
A millisecond is one thousandth of a second (1/1000)
A second is (1/86,400) of a day that means that there are 86,400
    seconds in one day
A minute is 60 seconds
An hour is 60 minutes
A day is 24 hours
A week is 7 days
A fortnight is 2 weeks
A month is 4 weeks
A quarterly is 3 months
A semi is 6 months
A year is 12 months
A decade is 10 years
A century is 100 years
A millennium is 1,000 years
A mega-annum is 1,000,000 years
A giga-annum is 1,000,000,000 years

A tera-annum is 1,000,000,000,000 years

An eon is an unknown amount of time, infinite

Time is a variable for everything in life. This book is highly mathematical. Math is critical to understand. Time is math. If you apply the math for yourself, you can break down any measurement of time.

You can say that a year is:

12 months

52 weeks

365 days

8,760 hours

525,600 minutes

31,536,000 seconds

31,557,600,000 milliseconds

31,536,000,000,429 microseconds

31,556,926,000,000,000 nanoseconds

I realize that the year may very slightly, altering my answers. For simplistic reasons, I am not going to do the math and define a year with alterations in the seconds such as tropical year, Gregorian year, Julian year, and such. The idea is to formulate intervals of time into greater or smaller segments. This chapter's purpose is to show the measurability of time.

Time is everything in this universe. Many people live through time but do not think about time. Time is the absolute greatest unit of measurability in this universe. Your existence and everything around you is the sum of time. It takes time to achieve greatness. Nobody has been great without putting in the time. Time makes people and breaks people. Time can be your greatest friend or your worst nightmare. Time is more important than money and any materialistic possessions because time cannot be replaced. Time is a great variable and everything is measured in time. Income, Relationships, Health, and Happiness are all measured in time.

People fail because they do not make their goals measurable. Goals without action and proper math measurement are simply wishes. People do not stop themselves from living in the past and that prevents them from living out their dreams and feeling ful-fillment. The measurability of time needs to be measured from right now to the future. Thinking about the past is measurable, but that measurement is already over. Measure from where you are now to where you want to be in the future. Without a set date or calculated approximation, you will not get what you want. Like anything, it is better to do it right now because later never comes. Deal with the pain now rather than dealing with a lot more pain later. Think of what you want to achieve and create a measurement.

Idea + Proper Math Measurability + Consistent Action + Time = Success

Time is the biggest factor in this mathematical equation. You can do something great one time, but if you do something great many times, it will eventually become even greater. You can talk all you want about something, but only time will tell. Time never lies. Time is a constant. Time is the truth. People lie but numbers never lie. You will know that yourself or someone is great because of the great time spent will speak for itself.

If you spend 1 hour learning something, you will know. If you spend 10,000 hours learning something, you will know more.

The quote, "The master has failed more times than the student has tried" is such a relevant quote to time. It is the number of little things that build bigger and better things over time. Big cannot be big unless it is first small. Small takes time to become big. Patience is a virtue and is a virtue of time. Always go back to patience. Nobody has the power to speed up time or to slow down time.

Time has a funny way of making time feel slower when bad decisions are made and of making time feel faster when good decisions are made. When you are having fun and enjoying things, time seems to be going really fast. When things are bad and you are constantly sad, time seems to be going really slow. When the mind changes, things may not be going really slow or really fast. Sometimes you may feel that time is not even passing. Time can make you wake up in a cold sweat and shock with great fear throughout you by how much time has passed. Time can make things better or worse.

Time goes forward and it does not go back. The seasons change as constant as time passes. If you want to be successful in life, you must learn how to adapt to your environment. The environment is always changing. The changes are derived from time. Time is changing things in business, in health, in relationships, in moods. Time waits for nobody. You must adapt yourself to time because time will not adapt to you. When time changes things and you are able to adapt, you will evolve. The reason that time changes things is because it is trying to evolve things into a new adaptation. It is up to you to evolve into new adaptations as the time changes. If you do not adapt to changes, you will not evolve. The primary reason for life is to evolve and to change things over time. Life reproduces new ideas and creates new conditions for things to live.

As time passes, it is important to not use excuses for the things that you think are controlling you. If you feel controlled by things, you will be unhappy. Time is in nature and your surrounding environment cannot control you. Only you can control yourself and your thoughts, interpretations, beliefs, perceptions, views. The changes are going to do what the changes are going to do and you can change the way that you want to feel about things. Find the alternatives of life because life over time always offers alternatives. You are way more in control of yourself than you think, regardless of time changes.

People do not realize that there is a time to fail and there is a time to succeed. There is a time to be sad and a time to be happy. There is a time to give and a time to receive. There is a time for everything and there is everything in time. Although it is important to have an abundance mindset in life, time is of the essence and it is scarce. Your time needs to be spent wisely. You will never have the same time again. You will never live that second again and you need to make the most of it by not wasting it on things that do not matter.

Every purchasing decision that you make is directly related to time. When you decide on purchasing something, you are emotionally calculating how long it took you to acquire the amount of money. People fear the loss of time. The fear of time lost is the biggest killer of dreams. People paralyze themselves with fear because they are scared that if they put in the time and they fail, that time is wasted. If you put in the time and you give it your all, time is never wasted. Especially if you loved what you were doing. You are in competition with nobody but yourself.

People are scared to leave a toxic or unhealthy relationship because of all the time that they had invested. It may logically be more beneficial for a person to leave the relationship than to be consumed by the fear of the time wasted. If you loved that person during any time in the relationship, then time was not wasted. People fear that if they fail in front of people, they will feel that their efforts have gone to waste. These are just stories and lies that we tell ourselves. Never care about what anybody thinks about your failures. They are your failures, not theirs. If you tried your best and failed, time was not wasted. Time is only wasted when you do not try or if you do not try again to succeed. If you have problems in life, do not fix the problem, fix your thinking and over time the problems will fix themselves.

If you want your situation to change, just imagine how much better it will be if you did it right now rather than allowing even more time to pass. Time is a very real thing. You should watch a clock one day and see it pass before your eyes, it is very moving to see. It is something that is perpetually moving parallel to your life and even after your life. You never know how long you have to live. Your genetics, lifestyle, health, environment, and many other variables can take you from existence into your grave. Today could be your last day to live, tomorrow could be your last day, next Tuesday could be your last day, one month from now could be your last day, one year from now could be your last day. Time is unforgiving and it waits for nobody. Compared to a trillion years, you are only here for a very short time on this majestic planet.

When your time is up, you are gone from existence. Your time on this planet is unknown. Live every day and moment like it is your last day to be alive.

Imagine dying tonight at midnight, what would you do differently? I bet that you would be doing a lot of things differently. If you were going to die at midnight, you would be able to recognize that you can completely change the actions of your life instantly. By knowing that you would be dead forever by midnight, you would have a major change in your actions. The fear of dying at midnight would not paralyze you because you would know that anything you do now would not matter tomorrow. Knowing this, you would just do what you love and not have a single care about the opinions of anybody. You would live every second up until midnight doing what you wanted the way that you wanted.

Maybe midnight is too soon. What if you knew that you were going to die exactly three years from today's date? You would not be the same person. You would live in the moment and make the maximum use of your time. The only components that give time purpose are continued existence and occurring events. Without those two, time would just be a pointless perpetuation of infinite numbers.

If you think hard enough and you have a crystal clear vision of what your ideal future will look like, you can be living your dream in space-time before you have lived it. If you are visionary enough to imagine your ideal life in the future, you are traveling through time. Time is limitless and a highly spiritual realm. Time is something that you cannot see, but time is always present. Time is beyond physical matter. Time heals absolutely everything. Pain is temporary and temporary is pain.

Time is very multidimensional because you can dream about a parallel universe. In a parallel universe, everything is completely opposite of what currently is reality. If you dream and believe hard enough, you can be living your ideal parallel universe in this reality. Imagine what your life would be like if you were in a parallel universe and you were living out your dream and feeling completely fulfilled. You have to use the dimension of time to see.

Time sees things that nobody can see, but if you look hard enough, you may see things before time reveals itself. Become a visionary of a better future. Time is the distance in between events. You could be living in your past, which is living in the dimension of time. Time and space are intertwined in perfect harmony. Time and space are a mathematical law of the world and they always Balance each other perfectly. Live in the dimension of space and time and imagine the changes that you could make to live the life of your most extraordinary dreams.

I know this sounds very spiritual, but spirit is necessary in this world and spirit is simply a mathematical force with the purpose of formulating results. If there were no spirituality, there would be no force to create evolution. The universe and everything in the universe is constantly evolving and that means you too. There are physical laws and there are spiritual laws. You can think of it as the spirit of time. Time is invisibly moving forever, yet we can feel its essence. Time does not fly but it floats like a spirit. Time is a very beautiful spirit and like any spirit, there is good and bad spirit, good and bad times in perfect harmony. Then there is the Balance between the spirits.

This planet that we are living on is revolving around the sun. That could easily be defined as a symbolism for time. The planet moves around the sun like the hands of a clock. Without the sun and the moon, our great ancestors would have not figured out the phenomenon of time using old devices such as sundials. Time is measured in frequencies. Everything in this universe has a frequency and frequency is mathematical. Frequencies are forces and forces are frequencies. As a human being, your time is under the human life span. The human life span is not very long.

It is wise to make the best use of your time with a calendar. When you use a calendar, you are implementing a great amount of math. Calendars are mathematical tools that help you complete goals, much like a hammer is used to hit a nail until the nail is in the desired spot. Calendars are more space-time oriented because there is no physical time in place. Clocks are physical and you can see a clock count time before you. Physical clock measurements are much smaller in comparison to a larger measurement from a calendar. The calendar can give you a more planned out blueprint of how you are going to spend your time and a physical clock will just help you with the day. Calendars are always going to be a more powerful mathematical tool to help you achieve your dreams, goals, desires, in comparison to the daily physical clock that will give you a guideline of the day.

When you learn to plan out your life with a calendar, then life will not be planning you out as much. Control or be controlled. Life is all about control and time grants the time in which you remain in control. Use control for good. You have a lot more control of your life than you think. Time will work with you if you learn about time. Time will work against you if you do not learn to take the time to get to know time. If you are really ambitious, get a device that monitors a calendar and clock at the same time. If you can plan every hour of your day, you will become much more productive. It is amazing how many people do not take the time to write things in a calendar. Your brain is tremendously powerful, however, it will not remember everything. Humans by nature forget things.

Time is inconsistent around the world. Everyone coexists in the same time and space, but time zones alter how different regions measure time. It is not the same time where you are currently reading this book as it is on the opposite side of the world where you live. Time may not be reality, but we use time in reality. Maybe time is an illusion of our imagination. I argue that without some mathematical measurement, you will not put the necessary pressure on yourself to take action towards your goals.

The past is fixed and will not change and the future is unfixed and can change. The movement of time is part of the mathematical laws of nature. You can change your whole life by taking interest and learning universally true laws of mathematics in nature. Study closely. Time is a constant and will never stop, even long after we are gone. Time starts once and never stops again.

When the brain's chemicals change, time may slow down or speed up, but remains the same in real time. The space-time remains the same, but the space-time feels different to the brain. In the minds of animals, they only think in the now and do not plan ahead. Humans are such evolved animals, that we are able to plan our lives for the future. Alterations to the mind make the judgment of time different. Use your sophisticated mind to create a new life for yourself by planning your life out. With daily planning, you will eventually realize your dreams.

People feel disappointed when things do not happen right away. People are very impatient and patience is a must to learn. People are uncalculated about their expectations of time and how long they have to wait before a desired occurrence happens. Things can happen a lot quicker than you may think and some things take a lot longer than you may think. The more calculated the estimate of time, the better and more educated the person's expectation of time may be. Sometimes however, it is not easy to formulate a precise amount of time before your desired something happens for you.

Everything will come back to your time management. As a human being, you need to fight your animal mind that is living in the moment and implement your more evolved human mind to plan your life. If you master time management, you will be successful in any field. If you have never wrote things in a calendar, take a week to see how your typical week looks like. Write down what time you wake up, when you eat, how much money you spend, when you go to bed, who you surround yourself with, when are you most busy, when are you least busy. See how long each thing takes you. There are so many variables from human to human. No two schedules are going to be identical and you need to find out what works for you. Go through the trial and error and master time management. Manage your time and do not let time manage you.

Time will reveal the behavior of yourself and others. You can learn so much about someone from watching their behavior over a period of time. Everyone is capable of concealing his or her natural behaviors only for a period of time. Over time, their nature will eventually come out. Study and see the progression of people, places, and things. Study patterns. Time changes things, even slightly. Nothing stays the same. The past may or may not repeat itself in a variation of what has happened before. Focus on the short term and long term. Look at the bigger picture and the details. Look for the stability.

Time management and calendars are stability for you. If you do not plan things out, you will have instability. The time that we live in is the busiest that it has ever been. Time is limited in today's world. Plan and schedule carefully. You can evolve your productivity by seeing in your calendar how you spent your time in the previous weeks or months. The management of time allows you to mentally organize your highest priorities and your lowest priorities. Your highest priorities should be the things that will help you evolve the most. Become spatially aware. Create the critical time lines that you need to reach your place of greatness.

Some cultures around the world write from left to right. Other cultures write from right to left. You can think about your past as writing from left and your future as writing towards the right. In other cultures, you can think about your past as writing from right and your future as writing towards the left.

Past . . . . .Future

Left . . . . Right

Future . . . . Past

Right . . . . Left

As you can see, the past and the future coexist simultaneously and are intertwined harmoniously. They remain a parallel and everything in life has a parallel energy to Balance it. For the good, there is the bad. For the really bad, there is the really good.

Understand that you will never find time for anything. If you want to have the time in your life, the only thing that you can do is to make time. Humans use their time so poorly and focus all of their time and energy on things that do not matter. Do not focus on things that do not matter. Most things around you do not matter. Focus on the good things that matter, because you know deep within yourself what the right thing to focus on is. Master your patience and time. Time is free to use and to spend, but time can be priceless.

Your time is your greatest commodity and your time is the greatest gift that you can give. Your time is more important than any of your material possessions or money. Nobody is too busy, including you. The importance level of your priorities is the only thing that will make you busy or not busy. Time will show you what matters. You may be visiting a building because someone built the building in time before. If the person did not put in the time to build the building, you would not be visiting the building. The same goes for you, you need to put in the time to see something built. Go out there and build your dreams.

Time is an illusion for many people. Everybody thinks that they have lots of time to do something, especially before big tests. The truth is, as the deadline approaches, you may realize that you had a lot less time than you had anticipated and therefore, you should always start now than later. Too much time eventually becomes not enough time if you do nothing about it. Ask yourself if the things that you did today are getting you closer to where you want to be, or further from where you want to be.

You will never be able to take back words that you have said, time that you have spent, and moments that you have lived. You must be very careful. Time is a very powerful energy. Your words, your actions, and your time are very powerful energy sources that can help you or hurt you a lot. Some things may help you gain time, and some things may set you back time. Your time and your life are one. It is better to master the two than to waste both of them. You create your future through your mind and you must take the proper action to realize your dreams.

In most cases, it is better to stop wasting time looking for something and start creating. However, seek and you shall find. When you look, you can find anything. When you have exhausted from looking, start creating. I want you to stop wasting your time on anything that is not fulfilling and you living out your dream because you are going to die. Remember that it is always better to be too early than too late.

Do not waste your time living through someone else's life. Too many people idolize someone or a group of people too obsessively and that takes time from living your life. It is okay to admire someone, but do not allow yourself to be too consumed in someone else's life. Live your own life. Believe it or not, you can be amazing just like your idol if you invest time in yourself to evolve. Never care about what anyone thinks about you if you love what you are doing. Remember the silence, and to silence the noise. When you can forget about having time and start making the time, you will become so much more productive.

Time is a luxury, time is delicate, time is scarce, and time is the best medicine. If you have ever been sick with the flu, time heals your sickness. Always work with time and not against time. When you create excuses and you procrastinate, you limit your time, causing you to work against time and time will win every time. If you did the best that you could, you did not waste time. The time is now and not later. Later never comes. Time is the best seed to plant, because when you plant a time seed, your time seed will grow into a major beanstalk.

Do not waste your time proving that you are good and worth a high value, just be good and of high value. Silence says a lot more than words do. You must be like time. Move like time. Fast like time. Forward like time. Move with time. Too late can happen at any time without notice, so it is better to act now than later. Time is always watching you, just as you watch time. If you waste time, time will waste you, if you work with time, time will work with you.

There is much insecurity engrained in so many of us that we waste our time trying to impress people. Spend your time with people that already like you. Not everyone is going to like you. Most people will not like you. The fewer people that like and appreciate you counter Balance all of the people that do not like you. If everyone liked you, what would be the point? Like attracts like and like repels dislike. Through time, you may have to go through the absolute wicked to get to the absolute wonderful. Be patient. Forgive and silence your pain. Move forward like time.

If you want to be a warrior with your time, follow this:

Plan
Use a Calendar
Know Deadlines
Learn to Say No
Focus
Arrive Earlier
Get a Watch
Use Alarm Reminders on Your Phone
Cut Out Distractions
Monitor Where Your Time is Spent
Prioritize
Complete Similar Tasks Together
Stop your Time Wasters
Actively Learn to Manage Your Time
Try New Systems That May Work Better
Stick to Your Plan

When you know something is right, the time to do it will always be right. If you know that you have a dream, your time to work towards achieving that dream is always going to be right. Time can be stressful. Breathe.

The time to get healthy is now
The time to get richer is now
The time to get love is now
The time to get happiness is now
The time to learn is now
The time to start is now
The time to work on your dreams is now
The time to eliminate toxic people and situations is now
The time to start a new life is now
The time to reinvent your self is now

It has always been the case. No matter what your situation is, it has always been the time for you. The time is now. It has always been now. You have the power to start now. Right now. Time is an illusion that you burden yourself with. Break the illusion and just start living your life now.

Stop waiting for time because time will never be waiting for you. Turn that fear volume dial in your brains stereo all the way down to mute. Annihilate your excuses. Diminish your self-doubts. Slaughter your procrastination. You are good enough and your time is now. Anything small in life is a smaller version of something big. Your dreams are a smaller version of your dreams being lived in reality.

Learn to value yourself highly. If you do not value yourself highly, you will not value your time. Until you value your time, you will not do anything great with it. If you do not value your time, other people will not value it either. Do not give away your gifts or talents for free unless it is for the greater good. If you give your time, talents, and gifts away for free, people will use you. Value yourself, your gifts, your talents, and your knowledge. Value you.

One Day . . . . Day One

Go From Here . . . . To Here

It really is that simple to make the switch in words and apply it to your life. When you flip one day to day one, day two will follow the next day. In life, you will need to change your thoughts and the problems will change. For every problem, there is a solution waiting to be discovered.

In business, nobody cares about your time or your feelings. They do not care about you. The only thing people care about is how valuable you can be to them. They will be willing to pay if you can make them better. The only thing that matters in business is value and how valuable you are. They do not care about your time, they only care about your value. The best way that you can spend your time in business is to start making yourself more valuable. When you become of great value, everything will follow.

Your marketing, your product, your service, the operations of the company, your prices, your reputation, everything is able to grow when you start by making yourself valuable. Valuing your time is the best way to start becoming more valuable. Business is the art of exchanging value. Of course time is a factor in business, you can save or lose a lot more time based on how valuable you are. Only through spending time on yourself, will you become more valuable. Work on new skills and develop new knowledge. If you are valuable enough, people will pave a way to your doorsteps. When you are valuable, the lineup out your front door may be longer than you could possibly imagine.

Living in time is a great thing, but burnouts do occur. When we spend a large amount of time working on something without proper rest and recharge, we will burn out. Burnout is the number one reason why people give up and fail in life. Without question, burnouts kill dreams if you do not recharge. Time is the only thing that will help you heal and recharge. Rest the mind, body, and soul.

Meditation has been around for a very long time and there is a reason why many people still use it today. You can recharge your mind with only 15 minutes a day of focused meditation. When you get up earlier, you will have more time in the day. Wake up early and meditate, it is hard at first, and then it becomes easy. All it takes is discipline. When you learn discipline, you will succeed. Taking action is a big part, but without discipline, you will fail. Find the best way that works for you in dealing with your burnouts. If you burn two ends of the candle simultaneously, eventually you will run out of wax. The same is true with working on yourself, your goals, your vision, and your desires. Find positive ways to recharge and ease your mind. Stress is a big reason why people have burnouts. The mind is able to focus for a long time, but not forever. Readjust your focus accordingly when your level of focus drops. Take healthy rests, and then continue forward.

Even writing this book, I am prone to burnouts. I love the process of writing this book because I want so many people to enjoy the messages in this book. I write completely out of love and I enjoy the process of writing more than the end result. I may run out of ideas or spend too much time physically writing. I recharge by meditating and by doing other things that I love. I may rest or take my mind off of writing. I will surround myself with nature and feel the calmness and the sound of silence. It is really funny that when I stop writing, ideas seem to flow to me unexpectedly. I discipline myself by writing a number of pages or I will allow myself so many days off of writing. I will look in my calendar and see what time I will start to write again. By taking the time to relax my mind, new ideas form and my level of focus feels replenished. I start writing again with a newfound high level of excitement and passion.

No matter how much you love something, doing it a lot will burn you out. If you had no burnouts and you could just go forever, what would be the point? Nature wants us to rest. When you start your day one, or if you are on day 700, take proper care of yourself. When you rest and recharge, you will perform much better, allowing you to evolve better, stronger, and quicker. The worst thing that you could possibly do for yourself and your dreams is to tell yourself that you are too tired, bored, or uninspired. Effective recharges will give you a new outlook and level of productivity.

Never give up, just take disciplined breaks. Take control of your breaks. Do not take too short breaks or too long breaks. You cannot be strong all the time. Feel sadness and fatigue sometimes, but when that is over, get back up. Anything that we do goes up and goes down, goes up and goes down. You will feel strength, then you will feel weakness, then you will feel strength again, and then you will feel weakness again. You will have successes, then failures, then successes, and then failures.

Over time,
Your health will go up, then down, then up, then down
Your wealth will go up, then down, then up, then down
Your love will go up, then down, then up, then down
Your happiness will go up, then down, then up, then down
Your energy level will go up, then down, then up, then down

The universal law of life is that things will be up, then they will be down, then they will be up, and then they will be down. That process carries on indefinitely in any matter in life.

When you are learning, you are never wasting your time. When you are evolving, you are not wasting your time. If something bad happened to you, but you learned through the process, you did not waste your time. The future comes one day at a time. The future and time are a slow, but forward moving process. 3 years from now will not be here until 3 years have passed. 10 years from now will not be here until 10 years have passed. One day at a time is how the future comes. By working hard, and working towards your goals one day at a time, you are essentially living in the future. What you do repeatedly is what you will eventually become. If you are doing the things now that you see yourself doing in the future, you are already creating that future. You are already starting to live that future vision. The future is far, but the future can start right now if you decide that the future starts now. If you read this book everyday, you will finish it in the future. If you just flip to the very last page of this book, you will already be living in the future. It is in your power to start living your ideal future.

Paying attention is the best skill that you can have. Pay attention to time. Most people lack attention. Attention means to focus. What are you focused on? What are you going to focus on faithfully? You can pay attention for a short amount of time, or you can pay attention for a long period of time. Attention is time. When you have little attention, you have little time. When you have a lot of attention, you will have a lot more time. When you pay attention to something, it will give a greater understanding and respect for something.

People now have very little time on focus attention the things that matter to them the most. Free up your time and you will have a lot more time to focus your attention. You have to prioritize and know what needs more attention and what needs less attention. Paying attention is a measurement of time. Some people study one thing and pay very close attention to just one thing and some people pay very close attention to many things during the course of their life. When you have no time, you have no attention. Make time and create more attention. It is all about making time.

Giving money is not as meaningful as giving your time. The greatest love that you can give to someone is your time. Even if you have no time at all, and you are still able to make time, that is the most divine form of love that you can give. Time makes people come into your life and go out of your life. Your purpose is to be happy. You never know how much time that you have to live. It is much better to die happy than to die miserable.

The purpose of time is to allow things to happen. Without time, things would happen too often or not often enough. Things may all happen at one time or not happen at all. Time allows the timeline for events to happen and everything happens for a reason. Time will create things and moments to happen. Everyone will change through time. Time is the core of evolution and helps people to evolve. Without time, there would be no mathematically logical evolution. People are going to change. In relationships, people over time may grow closer to each other or further from each other. There is no key to happiness. Happiness starts with you and your mind. You know deep down which things make you happy and which things make you unhappy.

Some people only see you when it is convenient and some people free up their time to see you. Know the difference and learn to know who is important in your life. Be around the people who are the most important to you. If you want to evolve, the people who you spend the most time with are a reflection of what you are most likely going to become. This is not always the case because there are exceptions to every rule, but whom you are around is generally a good reflection of yourself.

This may be a hard concept to grasp, but it is necessary to understand if you want change. Some people are completely toxic and hold us back intentionally or unintentionally. We stay friends with them because they are fun to be around and we have known them for so long. Sometimes family members may not be healthy to be around. Family is important, one of the most important things in the world. Be careful whom you spend your time with. You have a tendency to pick up some of their habits. Be careful of who has influence over you. Trust yourself. The best person to trust is you.

Surround yourself with people that are more evolved than you, people that you aspire to be. Surround yourself with people that help you grow and people that are positive. Negative people bring negativity out and positive people bring positivity out.

If you want to become richer, hang out with rich people

If you want to have a loving relationship, be around people in a loving relationship

If you want to be happy, be around happy people
If you want to be more fit, hang out with fit people
If you want to be smarter, hangout with smart people
If you want to be more skilled, hangout with people more skilled than you
If you want to make it, be around someone that has already made it

No matter what you want to become, surround yourself with people that have already become what you want to be. You are responsible for how you spend your time. Spend it well or spend it poorly. As time goes by, you will eventually die. Make the most of your time and let time bring you to your dreams. Time is measured in moments. Start doing things and creating moments. The time to start is now!

6

Purpose

Time to talk about your purpose in the modern world. Many people have a lack of identity and feel lost in their journey through life. They ask themselves, "Why am I here?" This is completely normal to question your existence and why you have been put on this planet. Especially when teenagers just finish graduating, they feel the most lost because all they knew was high school. They enter the big world with a sense of confusion and uneasiness.

Maybe you are older and you think that it is too late for you to pursue your dreams. You think it is too late because you already worked for a company for 30 years of your life. Remember that these are just stories that we tell ourselves and are completely untrue. Dreams are ageless and can be realized at any age. Deep down, you know what your dream is and why you were put here.

Instead of pondering in confusion, simplify your thinking. Your purpose is to be happy. That is the universal reason for everyone's purpose. What makes you happy is what makes your purpose unique to you. The first question that you need to ask yourself is "What do I love?" You should not have to think very hard about what you love because you already know what you love instinctually. After you have asked yourself what you love, ask yourself, "What would I do for free?"

Chances are, the thing that you would do for free is something that you are passionate about, like your hobbies. You are passionate about your hobbies because you love doing them. Hobbies can be anything. The next thing that you need to do is to figure out a way to monetize your hobby. In a nutshell, your purpose is to monetize something that you love doing. When you are passionate about a hobby, you will work incredibly hard on it because you love it and you believe in it. If you dislike what you do, the universe is telling you that the thing that you are doing is not your purpose. Your purpose is doing the thing that you love because that is what is going to bring you happiness and fulfillment. When you do something that you do not love, you will not work as hard at it. If you are not putting everything into something, you are wasting your time. You need to be pouring your heart and soul into something that you love.

Your hobbies may include: Acting, Racing, Radio, Baking, Swimming, Skateboarding, Books, Coloring, Cooking, Writing, Dance, Drama, Drawing, Electronics, Embroidery, Sports, Fishing, Skating, Building, Magic, Painting, Photography, Music, Sculpting, Comedy, Video Games, Movies, Yoga, Astronomy, Bodybuilding, Camping, Diving, Flying, Blacksmithing, Martial Arts, Graffiti, Horse Riding, Biking, Paintball, Rafting, Rock Climbing, Rugby, Football, Shooting, Skiing, Traveling.

There are an endless amount of things that you could be passionate about. You may be passionate about many things or just one thing. If you do not know what you love, do things that you really like to do because odds are, it will bring you to something that you love. If you do things that you do not like, more times than not, you will not find what you love.

The time that you are living in is the modern time. You may or may not know it, but the modern time is where you have to be to live out your passion. The modern time is the digital age. Everybody has access to the Internet. Everybody is consumed with the modern phenomenon of social media and it is here to stay. It will be here after you die and long after that. It is the way that people communicate now. Earlier in this book, I talked about taking effective resets from social media, as it is necessary to get off social media sometimes. The truth however, is that if you want to live out your purpose and succeed in modern business, you are going to have to use social media. There are many social media sites, but the most important ones are Facebook, Twitter, Instagram, and YouTube. Social media may change and the importance of each site may vary over time. For the next while, I do not see these sites becoming irrelevant.

In the modern world, it is completely acceptable to have a full-time job on social media. People are becoming personal brands and anyone can create their own clothing line. You can start any business that you want on social media. The thing that makes social media optimal for you to live out your dream and purpose is because social media sites are a free advertising source. That is exactly right, social media is free marketing. You are able to market yourself, your business, your brand, your hobbies, your life, any-thing and everything can be documented on social media. Most people today do not realize the power and influence that social media plays in the modern world. That influence and power of social media can be in your favor if you master it.

A long time ago, if you had an idea you would need to spend a lot of money if you wanted to see it come to life. It was much harder to become seen in the public eye and to have your thoughts come into fruition. Now, a 10 year old could become a millionaire on social media. Build your brand on social media by document-ing your hobby and gaining an audience. When there are enough eyeballs on you, you can monetize that. Money follows attention. Now, you do not have to update your resume to go and work for somebody. If you do what you love and let people see your love for something, you will create an audience for yourself. When there is an audience, there is greater opportunity for you because you never know who could be watching. Anyone in the world could be watching. Of course, as with anything in life, there is good and bad with social media. Social media offers much more good than bad.

On a social media platform, it is one giant community with the world. Anyone can contact you and you can contact anyone. Anyone can become a personal brand. You can talk to anyone you admire. It may be harder to get into contact with some people than others, but anything is possible. If you have a bigger audience, it is much easier to get into contact with certain people.

Before, you needed to get on TV to promote yourself or your business. Now, TV is becoming extinct and more people are tuning into online media. Now, anyone can become famous and share their talents and gifts with the world. One video may go viral and then your life will never be the same. You could become a movie star right out of your garage. Imagine the millions of people that could watch you perform your greatest passions. Having a big audience watching you may inspire other people to live out their dreams and it spreads like wild fire. On social media, like attracts like and you may be exposed to other artists, or people similar to you who share your interests. You could make friends or find a romantic relationship on social media.

If you post a picture of an old car that you are passionate about, someone on the Internet may like the picture of your old car and reach out to you. They may send you a message and you could make a new friend with a mutual interest, all because of you posting a picture of something that you are passionate about. In my personal life being on social media, I have had people follow my page with similar interests as me. When I click on their profile, I may be inspired, learn something, or engage in a pleasant conversation with them. Generally, what you post on social media, you will receive attention from people based on similar interests. Social media is a place where you can inspire and get inspired. It is a place where you can teach and you can learn. It is a place where you can connect with other people and gain new perspectives from other people about your passion. If you see somebody do your passion in a different way than you do it, it may inspire you. The inspiration may cause you to try a new way and make you become better at the thing that you love.

All you need is a little confidence and to put yourself out there. In your wildest dream, you may create an audience of millions of people who are watching you daily. Out of the millions of fans, one person may have a company and they may want you to promote their product on your page. The person may offer you $1,000, $5,000, or it could be a much more lucrative amount than that. You just never know. They may wire the money straight into your account via PayPal instantly. You get paid while doing the thing that you love most. The greatest thing in life is to do something that you love really well and to receive some recognition for it. When people offer you money for your gifts and talents, that is one of the greatest recognitions that you can receive.

The reason that I am saying that you should do what you love and monetize it is because you still have to earn a living somehow. In a perfect utopia world, where money did not exist, then you would just do what you love. In this world, money is important and you have to earn it. You may as well earn your money doing what brings you happiness and fulfillment rather than something that brings you misery and sadness. Lots of people sacrifice their happiness for a bigger income. The truth is, that if you earn a smaller income and you are happy, that is true riches. When you achieve that sustainable happiness, that is what makes you successful. Money does not measure your worth or your level of success. Money only measures your worth and success in business. In a spiritual world, doing what you love is the thing that makes you successful.

Everywhere you go, no matter where, people have money. All of these people with money are on social media. The richest people and the poorest people go on social media. The smartest, most talented, most successful high achievers go online. Anyone of them can see your genius mind engage in the love for your craft. Do you really need that extra income and be miserable at your job just to have a fancier car any a bigger house? When you love what you do, it will not feel like work and you will work hard at it. You may not feel the immediate desire to travel if you love what you are doing. There is absolutely nothing wrong with wanting more, but there is an amount of income that is sustainable enough to be happy. Numbers are infinite and if you focus your happiness on numbers, you will never be happy because numbers are limitless.

Do what you love and you will always have what you want. In life, true fulfillment and happiness from doing what you love cannot be bought. It is priceless. $150,000 a year and completely miserable is not going to make you as happy as $75,000 a year and doing what you love.

Now this is going to be tough for a lot of people, but it is necessary. There will be some point in your life where you are going to have to take a chance. There is going to be a point, where you need to quit your day job and just go for it. Go for your passion. I am not telling you to quit your day job and be homeless. Make sure that you are covered. Do not quit your 9-5 job until your passion is making you money. Do your passion on the side of your 9-5. Digest the idea that at some point, if you want to pursue your dream and live your purpose, you are going to have to roll the dice and just go for it. There is nothing wrong with a 9-5 job, but a steady paycheck that is nice and comfortable is not going to be worth your happiness. You need to live in a period of discomfort to reach a higher level of comfort for yourself.

You need to put all your eggs in one basket. Think about who is at the top of where you want to be and realize that anything is possible. You can be right up there with them. All you have to do is put your mind to it and have a plan. Nobody may know who you are, but if you give it some time, you will see that people will start to hear about you and watch you. You can come from absolutely nowhere and have an audience watching you live out your greatest passions. This is not fantasy or fiction, this is completely real talk. If you can perceive something, you can achieve something. If it is in your mind, it can become real. If what I were saying were a lie, there would be no inspirational people. There would be no famous people, no rich people, and no talented people. There are all of the things that I just mentioned in reality. You can become one of those things if you just document the thing that you love most and share it to the world. Share your talents and gifts because the world is waiting to see. You just never know, you never know. No matter how big your goal may seem, just plug away and you will get a lot further than you could possibly think of in a short amount of time. You just never know, who knows?

It will not take a lifetime and it will happen a lot faster than you may think if you put in the work and you are good at what you do. You have to be good at what you love to do to really live out your purpose. Put in the time to be great. You are going to be all in or all out in anything that you do in life. Excel at one thing better than anyone in the world and your world will be very dream like. Sometimes your purpose may change over time because things are always changing and evolving. Time evolves everything. Being happy is the stabilizer for your purpose. Your change of purpose simply means doing something else that you love and that makes you happy.

In life, the natural progression for anything is start easy, then progress harder. Most people are too hard too quickly and burn out. They burn out and then they give up. Burnout is the second biggest reason why people fail, because they do not recover from their burnout and give up. The number one reason why people fail is because they are scared, particularly of what other people are going to think and say about them. Fear talks them right out of trying. If you have to think about what you are doing, you are doing the wrong thing. When you love something, you will naturally do it.

Think about the moon for a moment. The moon is a mysterious glowing light that shines above us every night. No matter how rich you are, how poor you are, how talented you are, every human being on this planet is capable of looking at the moon. The idea that everyone can look at the moon no matter who you are is proof that if anyone has achieved something great, then you can achieve something great too. There is no alternative for hard work. Hard work breeds luck, the harder that you work, the luckier that you will find yourself.

Everything that you need to know about someone is in his or her eyes. When someone loves what they do, you will see it in their eyes. Their eyes will glitter and twinkle brightly. When someone is not passionate about something, his or her eyes will faintly dim. If you did something in front of a mirror that you love, you would notice your micro expressions change. Look into someone's eyes when they do something because the eyes give everything away. A person's eyes will show the level of love that they have for something. When the eyes resist something, the eyes are telling you more. You can see resistance and fear in eyes and that will tell you a lot about somebody's thoughts. The eyes will appear a lot gentler when there is love and honesty.

Do not focus on what the world is, focus on what the world can be. Imagine. Think about if failure were not an option, what would that look like to you? How would you show the world your passion? Would you do more of what you love? The idea is to ask your self what is possible. What if? Use your imagination because your imagination is limitless.

In entrepreneurship, many people spend time focusing on where the money is. The better solution is to focus on where the money is going to be. Use your imagination and think crazy. Keep your crazy idea fresh until it is an obvious idea. When you have unease, you create disease. Get rid of your unease and embrace crazy. When you think crazy, you are at ease and you will not develop disease. To think crazy is to think healthy. When you think healthy, you will be healthy. It is unhealthy to limit your mind and your creative expression. Humans were designed to create. Life is about creation and reproduction.

The definition of success is not about how much money you have, success is about how many lives that you have positively impacted. Do not worry about the money for the short term. When you do what you love, the money will follow you long term. Focus on sharing your talents, gifts, hobbies, and the thing that you love to impact the lives of people. You are being selfish to not share with the world the thing that you are most passionate about, especially because it will make a positive impact on many people's lives.

Life is a dream and it is what you make it. Do not optimize around exceptions, optimize around the general rule to point you in the right direction. You will never be successful if people do not like you. Not everybody is going to like you, but you cannot achieve success by yourself. Ironically, if you do not have people hating you, you are not doing something right. The next emotion to love is to hate. When people are spending their time hating you, it is because they are talking about themselves. What they say has nothing to do with you. Most people in the world have a poor mindset and they hate people that achieve success. When people are jealous, it means that you are becoming successful and better. Do not deliberately do things to make people hate you, but realize that hate is an indication that you are doing something right.

The point is that you need a certain number of people that like you and a certain amount of people that do not like you to become successful. If everybody liked you, what would be the point? If everybody hated you, what would be the point? Nobody hates for no reason, there is always a reason. Make that reason because you are successful. People may dislike you very strongly and become mean, ignore it. There may be a time and a place where you will need to stand up for yourself, but hatred is just meaningless noise. A hater's mission is to get a rise out of you to feel like they are somebody. Haters would do a backflip in excitement if you acknowledged them and gave them the time of day. People love to hate and hate to love. Remember that winners never hate and haters never win. Winners never complain and complainers never win. Successful people want others to win and unsuccessful people want others to lose.

Maybe your purpose is not on social media and it is in a more reclusive setting. Maybe you want to create a non-digital purpose for yourself and that is okay too. Though, social media in this modern time is generally a good place to start. Your purpose is your purpose and no two purposes are identical, only the foundation. The foundation of purpose that every one shares is to live a life that makes them happy.

No matter your purpose or how you are going to achieve your dreams, remember that it is not about the vision, it is about the execution. Too many people ponder and are waiting for the right time. The right time never will come. There will never be a right time. The right time is now and it has always been the right time. Too many people seek inspiration, get inspired, and remain inspired. Inspiration is great, but without execution, you are wasting your vision. Doing is almost always better than thinking. As execution is key, if people do not think that you are crazy, then that means that you are not dreaming big enough. Dream big, execute bigger.

Your brain is very logical and sees Black and White. The brain and the mind do not see the grey. The gut and your gut feelings will tell you when something does not feel right. The brain logically makes sense in terms of Black and White, but your gut instinct and intuition will tell you the grey, which is the Balance. Feeling can be more powerful than logic at times. The heart will tell you what the mind cannot. Follow your gut instinct and you will be on the right path.

We live in a twenty-four hour a day world. Business is twenty-four hours a day. In a day, there are only twenty-four hours. Every second that you breathe, you are living in business time. When you are sleeping, somewhere there is somebody working. When you are sleeping, other people around the world are developing their passion and doing the things that they love. The world is very loud and busy. The world is never silent. The biggest problems in the world are social problems. Problems create opportunity. Go for your dreams no matter what. Go for your dream even if you have no idea how it is going to happen.

Understand the power of leverage and duplication and you will succeed. In social media, duplicate your followers and you will increase your followers. Become live on a show and the show will duplicate viewers and you will get paid. If you have people's attention and eyes, you can monetize. Duplicate your skill into employees and you will be paid. Multiply your efforts, not your work. Like in business and money:

Duplicate $1 into $2, $2 into $4, $4 into $8 and keep going
Scale from 1 into 2, 2 into 4, 4 into 8, 8 into 16 and keep going.

Everything is duplication, learn the art of duplication through numbers and mathematics and things will become different for you.

Through your purpose, do not be arrogant. Success comes from not having to tell people who you are. Be humble. When you are humble, you open your mind to a whole greater potential and possibilities for new ideas. Give your gifts. If you cannot pay back, you can pay it forward. Your thoughts and your mind are a highly magnetic force. Your mind attracts what it thinks. When you change your mind, you change the people around you.

Your belief is everything. Get rid of toxic belief and have certainty in your belief. When you create doubt in your belief, it makes it less possible for you to achieve. Not anybody else, but you. Turn your disbelief back into belief. Do not watch history happen, make history happen. You have the power to make history if you apply your power. Everyone has a super power and your super power is capable of making history happen. When you think about what is possible, you attract the people that can help make it possible like a magnet. You can be good or you can be great. The choice will always be yours. There is a good way to do something and there is a great way to do something. Never sacrifice your integrity and values to get something. Always be true to yourself. Your needs will become different over time as everything evolves including your purpose. Everyone knows the good way and the bad way. Some act on the good and others act on the bad.

It does not matter how you view government, education, health care, war, the law, or anything that you feel may be a broken system. If you dream big enough, even you may be able to change things that you think are unjust, unfair, or you want to see differently. Do not let anything be a reason for you to create an excuse for yourself. Things may have not helped you, but at the end, the only thing that matters is if you help yourself. You can change you, that is what you have control of for certain.

Knowledge will always be power. Knowledge is powerful because the more that you know, the more that you will see. Learning is one thing, but you also have to learn efficiently. The day that you stop learning is the day that you die. You will not physically die, but you will become a spiritless zombie. Make people thirsty for your love and passion. If you show the world what you love, you will inspire them to learn. To learn is to evolve. People were put on this planet to create. Intellectual curiosity makes people thirsty to learn. Without the thirst of curiosity, there would be no point for someone to want to learn.

There is more than one way to learn things and different people learn things differently. There are more ways to love something than just one way. We all do slight variations of things. No two humans are identical. Keep in mind possibilities, big dreams, and never giving up. You will only fail if you give up. When things do not work out, it is simply a stepping-stone for a bigger idea and something that will work. In anything that you learn, you do not have to be a master immediately. Learn the basics. The basics will always take you a much longer way than you may think. Even if you are advanced, going back to the basics at times may be beneficial for you. Once you grasped the basics and understand them, then you can branch out and explore deeper. Things will always make more sense when you learn about something.

Your self worth is nothing of what you own, your self worth is from what you have created. If you own a lot and have not done anything, you are currently of no help to society. You can change that. Doing what you love and offering your talents and gifts to the world is creation. Through that creation, you are building your self worth. If you are a singer and the beauty and power of your music heals many people, that is what is going to make your self worth. The more people that you heal through your music, the greater your self worth becomes. If you are passionate about your organic product line that you sell and you help people to become healthier, then your self worth will be high. If you are producing no benefits to the world and are not trying to make the world better through your talents, gifts, words, products, or something beneficial, your self worth will be low and you are currently wasting your time here. Help evolve the world or else devolution will occur.

The reason that social media is essential to your purpose is because it is technology. Technology is a tool that you use to project your love and passion about something to the world. Since the majority of the world is on social media, it is essentially society. If you can help many people through social media, it will make a great impact on society, if your talents, gifts, love, passion is used for good. The formal name is social media but I call it society media. Social media is a lens of society. Society is one big community on social media platforms. There are two worlds on this planet, there is online reality and there is offline reality. There are online businesses and offline businesses. There are two forms of currency. There is the physical fiat money currency and there is the non-physical crypto money currency. The two worlds are intertwined into one. Social media will help supercharge your dreams and intertwine them with reality just like the online and offline world is intertwined. Dreams can become reality pretty quickly. There are so many social media accounts that nobody heard of that eventually became something. 0 can become 1 pretty quickly. Binary is always changing.

You need to be crystal clear about your goals and what it is that you want to accomplish on social media. The vision will give you direction and the execution will be the steps taken in the direction. Destinations are always reached when one step is put in front of the other. The best quality you can have is the intellectual curiosity to figure out how your dreams are going to come to life. When you go to bed, ask yourself, "Am I emotionally, spiritually, or intellectually better?" If not, work twice as hard the next day. Emotion, spirit, and intelligence are the three things that will create your life. It is always more fascinating to see how people think, not what people do. Do not follow rituals or habits, but follow thought processes. Doing other people's rituals will not help you as much as learning people's thought processes. What people think and what people do are not always congruent.

Always be who you are. Do not let anyone mold you into something else. Do not change to fit society. Stay crazy, because the crazy are the ones that change the world. The most successful men and women of all time have acted on their crazy idea and it changed the world for the better. Never stop learning. True greatness is finding happiness in your self. Learn about all of the things that you are not. Some people in life are naturally parasites and are toxic. Some people just read a script and play their part. That is their purpose. The world is a stage and each of us is an actor. You can read a script and play a role or you can create your own script and create your own role. Social media is the stage that we are all acting on. If you are not on social media, you are not on the stage. Create your part because it is your destiny. Everyone wants to see your talent and love.

Most people nowadays are offended by almost everything. Do not let things offend you and take things for what they are. If someone is offensive, just walk away and do not say anything. Only speak up if violence results because of offence. Try and understand why something may be offensive or where the person that is conveying the offensive message is coming from. Most of the time people that are offensive are not good people. Some people may have opposing arguments and beliefs than you. If someone is being civil about the different beliefs that they have, you should not be offended. If someone has a different political view than you and they are civil about it, you should not take offence to that person.

Everything can potentially be offensive, but everything should not offend you. If someone has pink hair, it should not offend you because it may be an eye sore to you. If the person with pink hair feels good about themselves and is not harming anybody, what is the problem? The point that I am making is that we live in a very soft world nowadays. People need to toughen their skin and not take things to heart. There were wicked diseases a long time ago during medieval times such as the black plague. The black plague was a harsh reality that affected many people. Now, people are so affected by simple words. Words should not hurt you.

If something is offensive and is a self-expression of someone else who does not promote physical violence, look away and ignore. Things are only going to get more politically correct and offensive and you need tough skin. The reason that I bring up the many people offended in today's society is because a lot of those offensive opinions are on social media. On social media, there are groups that are offended by everything. People create groups against things and most of the time it is a complete waste of energy. If people were as productive as they were in unproductive things, the world would be a lot better place.

The idea is that you should not care whether or not you offend people if the content that you are putting out is not directly bullying someone. Suppose that your greatest passion is erotic artwork and that you want to make a social media page with photos of your artwork. Contained in your artwork are paintings of the male or female genitalia with a psychedelic background. As long as it is legal and does not incorporate things such as child pornography or any other unlawful images, there is absolutely nothing wrong with posting it. If people's comments are homophobic comments of your artwork or other sly comments, then that is their loss that they could not appreciate the beauty in your artwork. If you love it, it does not matter what people think. For everything that is not liked and appreciated, there are other people that will like and appreciate something. Never worry about what people comment or say about you. You can delete comments or ignore their words. You see, hatred and people being offended stems from insecurity within themselves. If you are offended or hate something, it is because you are not secure in yourself about a particular subject or matter.

The thing that you are most passionate about and that you love should be shared on social media. You have no control if someone will be offended or not so what does it matter? If the passion, gift, talent that you share is from a place of love, forget about other people's biases. You cannot please everybody. Do not care what other people think, say, or feel about what you love and what you want to share with the world. It is your purpose that you are living, not theirs. Your purpose will take you to the place of your dreams where you will find contentment, peace, and fulfillment.

Of course, think before you speak and watch what you say. Say what you feel and say it from a place of love and you will not lose. Listen more and talk less. Make people feel that you care about them and what they have to say. You do not own words until you say them out loud. Be careful what words that you want to own. Accept the fact that you cannot help everybody and some people do not want to be helped. Whether people want to be helped or not, always do things from the place of greater good. The greater good is always the right way.

The most authentic form is from the place of love. Live out your passion, talents, gifts and the things that you love to be true to yourself and to the world. If you look at other people's pages on social media, remember that is their purpose and they are sharing the things that they love. If you decide to appreciate the gifts and talents of other people's pages, make sure to send empowering and loving comments. When you spread love, not only do you strengthen their purpose, you strengthen yours as well. After all, the purpose of life is to give. To give makes you happy.

You will always be happier when you give rather than receive. Your purpose is to give and that is to give the world your gifts, talents, and to praise others. Give your love to other people. When you spread hatred to other people, you are taking away from the beauty that they possess. Hatred is taking from others and taking away your self worth as a human being. When you give your love and compassion to others, you are giving and that is to live out your purpose. When you are living out your purpose, your dreams will be realized. The more you give, the more that you will receive directly or indirectly. Do not give for the sake of receiving because that is unauthentic and unloving.

Receiving is a by-product of your loving giving. Always approach a situation as to what you can give, rather than what you can get from a situation. You will not want to take more from a situation, but you will want to give more. You can only give time and you cannot receive time. The universe indirectly tells us that we need to give. Giving praise is better than receiving praise.

Social media allows you to share your message with the world. Your message can go viral. If something needs to be addressed, you can address it to society media. Maybe there is a special cause that you would like to make known. Maybe there is a secret that would like to share with the world that will change their life like it changed your life. Maybe you would like to pay it forward to send a message of giving. Maybe you want to voice something that should no longer be silent. Whatever your message is, no matter how big or how small, it can be heard. If two people hear your message, four people may hear your message, then eight people may hear your message, until the whole world knows your message. Give your message to the world. Address to be addressed.

You may already have a successful business running on social media. Find new ways to have more intimate and personal connections to your clients and customers. There are so many ways that you can create a higher level of engagement with your customers, clients, fans, and audience. You can gain instant feedback twenty-four hours a day. You can engage people via messages. All it takes is a little creativity. People can tell you what they think about your products, services, and organizations. All you need to do is listen through silence and you can ascend. Listen to what people say.

If you had a green shirt on and asked a complete stranger what color your shirt was, they would tell you that your shirt is green. The stranger might specifically say what type of green it is. They may say, "That shirt is lime green" People want to listen to what you have to say and people want you to listen to what they have to say. People love to give you their opinion. It is cool to have an opinion. People have the innate desire to be helpful. Nobody will tell you that your product or service is bad if it helps him or her. People will tell you right away if your product or service is bad without question. You can ask your existing audience to give referrals.

There is a lot you can come up with if you just apply yourself. Social media gives insights because you can learn about your competitor's products or services and see how you can do something better. Social media is a massive collection of data and if you use the data properly, it can be in your favor. Some data is unimportant and some data is highly important. Data is information and numbers do not lie. You can see post engagement levels by the number of comments and likes. Some social media sites tell you the age range of your followers and where people are located. This is all valuable information if you want to market effectively. Everything is right before your eyes. Do the proper investigation work and things will click for you. You will find that everything goes back to mathematics and numbers.

Social media allows people to promote their page and to put themselves in front of a larger audience. Social media may make you a financial fortune if you learn. Like anything, if you want to know something, become best friends with it. If you want to know social media, become best friends with social media. The more that you learn and know about your friend social media, the better off the friendship will be. No matter what your feelings are about social media and your purpose, social media is a whole new world that can make your dreams become a reality. There is good and bad with everything. Social media will always have more pros than cons. Social media is a skill that everyone should master in this modern digital age that we live in. Share your gifts, talents, passion, and hobbies with the world because the world is waiting to know who you are.

Happy journeys in the world of social media intertwined with your purpose to live out your biggest dreams. And remember, content is king!

7

Vision

Without a vision, you will not have a blueprint to map out your dreams. Your vision becomes your map. You will feel lost in time if you do not create a map of the future. When you are able to execute your vision into reality, you will feel your life become extraordinary. Visualize your dreams and form good habits. Consistency is the only way that your vision will be realized. When you own up to everything that happens to you instead of complaining, you will feel a lot more in control of your life. Envision the future. You may not know exactly how you are going to get there, but if you have the end goal in mind, you will get there. Creating a vision makes you one step closer, compared to not having a vision to begin with.

Imagine what completing your vision and dreams would look like, sound like, taste like, smell like, and feel like. How would it emotionally feel? If you can imagine it, you can live it. The two biggest components for completing any vision are innovation and marketing. Things are rarely always going to go your way and you will need to learn to adapt when things do not go as planned. Keep the end goal of your vision in mind and you will get there through trial and error. When creating a vision, think about everything that can go right and do not focus too much on what can go wrong. Every costly mistake is preventable.

It does not matter what people think about your vision except for yourself. When you vision, vision in a quiet space and vision positively. Positive visions end up coming into reality positively. When you think about your vision, make the vision of great value. Do not create a vision of evil because there is a lot of chaos in this world already. Humans need to learn that the real enemy is hatred itself and the way to find happiness is through unconditional love. Make your vision through unconditional love. There is so much quiet desperation in people. People are living and only existing in the workweek and not living their vision. Envision a better life. In your vision, never conform to everyone else and what people want you to be. You always must be yourself. Society will try and break your vision and your dreams, do not allow anyone to get the upper hand on you and make you like everyone else.

When you envision it, life will bring forward the right people, the right events, and things will synchronize into place. The universe is majestic and magical. After all, the world is great frequencies and forces. When you envision it, relentless consistency and action will get you to the end. Visions are fictional until you make them non-fictional. Nobody will vision for you and save you except for you. Do not wait for anybody to help you create your vision because it is your vision. Go look in the mirror at yourself and tell yourself that your vision is achievable and that you will do it. You will create a plan and you will take action to complete your vision.

Every great idea started because of a thought in the mind. Every great idea started in the brain above the shoulders and was carried out into physical existence from abstract existence. One thought passed through the mind and was built from non-existent to existent. Commit to your vision even if you do not feel like it. Even if you have a headache or are sick, you must commit to your vision. Through achieving your vision, you will fail. It is not a maybe that you will fail. When the vision that you create is bigger, you are going to fail more. More obstacles will be present to trip you up. When the visions are smaller, you will fail less. Failure is always a better teacher than success. Create a big vision to fail more and learn more. You do not learn anything through success. Body language is a great indicator of success and for your vision.

Keep a strong belief of certainty and strong body language that suggests confidence in your vision. If your body language is not aligned with your certainty of completing your vision, there will be a discrepancy.

As facial micro expressions are the number one indicator of a person, the second is body language as a whole. Body language is the secondary sign of a person's state and condition. You can learn a lot about someone through body language. Most communication is non-verbal. Verbal words play just a small role in communication. Actions always speak louder than words. Promises mean nothing until the actions back it up.

While achieving your vision, it is important to become aware of whom you associate with. The people around you are mirrors of yourself. Get the best people that you can possibly be around in your life. Ideally, you will want to be around someone who is older, wiser, more talented, more experienced, and more successful than you are. Who you aspire to be like is whom you should be around. Hunt for the best people to surround yourself with and eliminate toxic, dramatic people out of your life. Failures breed failures. Successes breed successes.

What we see may not be and what we do not see may be. Things that we see may change and what changes we may not see. There is a reason that there is such thing as déjà vu. You may have seen something in your mind while awake and conscious. You may have seen something in your dream while sleeping and unconscious. Make your déjà vu conscious and purposeful. Make the déjà vu exist because of your past vision. Déjà vu your visions and see it all before.

Flip your mindset that pain is pleasure and pleasure is pain. Enjoy the pain to enjoy the pleasure. When there is no pain, there is no growth. Only pleasure will not evolve anything. Evolution is directly a result of destruction and breaking down something before it evolves into the new evolved state. If you can enjoy the pain, you will achieve a heightened sense of spirit. If you sit on pleasure too long, pain will increase in the future. If you sit on pain too long, pleasure will increase in the future. Take steps gradually towards your goals. When you create a vision for yourself, it needs to have an emotionally compelling reason why you want your vision. If you do not feel emotional about your vision, it is not big enough or it is not a good vision. Your vision should ignite your soul with burning passion and make you feel swarmed with love. Your vision should move you and make you want to jump out of bed in the morning to work towards your dream.

The greatest emotionally compelling stability that you can have is your why. Why do you want your vision? If you do not have a reason, how are you going to believe in it? You need a stable foundation to believe in order to propel you forward in your vision's journey. Visions are future based and you need to put your mind into the future. Carry out present tasks to achieve future results and desires. You can live in the future if you consistently live what you want to be. Being lazy is a conscious choice that people make, so change it.

You are in control of your vision. You are the author and creator of your life. If your visions were not able to come to reality, you would be a tree. Focus on the outcome of your vision and reverse engineer the outcome to allow yourself to visualize what steps that need to be taken next. Pleasure is doing, pain is doing nothing. The pleasure is the pain and the pain is the pleasure. The pleasure is painful but the pain will bring out pleasure. The pain is pleasure but the pleasure will bring out pain.

It does not matter how fast that you do something, as long as you are making progress. Working fast and efficiently is essential, to get ahead but you need to master slow before you can master fast. Your actions are a lot more important than your words. Words can be lethal if you are not careful. Actions mean many words. Words can mean nothing.

The only thing that you are lacking is an idea, a vision. Deep down, you know what your biggest dream is. You are just scared. Get rid of the fear and work towards your vision. You are one vision away to create a better quality of life for yourself. Visions are much like wishes because visions can be created if you carry the wish out. Your visions are your wishes and you can make your wish come to life. You are the genie of your life. Every diamond needs to be cut before it becomes really beautiful. Your vision is the diamond and you need to cut the diamond. Cut the rock until a statue is evolved. Vision what the statue will look like and start working.

Do not let anyone take something away from you. Stand up for what you believe in. No one can take your vision away, unless you do nothing about your vision. Hatred is a reflection of someone else, not you. If you have a vision and people criticize your vision, they are just letting you know that they are insecure because they do not have a vision like the vision that you have. People become jealous of other people's visions especially when someone acts on their vision. People make themselves feel better about themselves by putting other people down, but their insecurities do not go away. Always keep your vision from a place of love. Touch it, feel it.

Ask yourself questions. How will this world be like? How will I feel emotionally? How strong are my beliefs? How can I implement the best strategy towards my vision? Make necessary changes. The idea is to envision. Look directly into your crystal ball and paint a mental picture of how it is going to look. The most successful people of all time were able to envision their dreams. Then they achieved them. You are able to envision. Be the visionary that you are.

If I said to you, "Imagine yourself wearing a hat." You would absolutely be able to picture in your mind yourself wearing a hat. It is just as easy to envision a big dream, as it is easy to envision a small dream. If I said to you, "Imagine a bigger balance of money in your bank account," you would absolutely be able to picture in your mind your balance of $5,000 and adding another 5 to create the number $55,000.

If I said to you, "Imagine yourself being on your favorite talk show host's studio with them," you would absolutely be able to picture yourself sitting on their chair and looking into their eyes with the studio audience. If you are single and I said to you,

"Imagine meeting someone that complements your life and is your ideal partner," you would start imagining what they look like, how much joy you would feel if you met your perfect match, what type of things you may do together, what values that you would share.

If I said to you, "Imagine creating a personal blog on social media that made you unbelievably famous," you would absolutely be able to imagine 1,000,000 views and up. You would imagine all the likes on your pages, all the emails sent to you, all the comments on your videos, all the fans that adore you. There is a saying that the sky is the limit, I say that there is no limit at all. If the sky is the limit, the galaxy is the unlimited. If you can envision it, it can become real. It can also become real a lot quicker than you may think.

If I said to you, "Imagine losing weight," you would absolutely be able to imagine getting rid of your clothing that does not fit you anymore because you will now fit smaller clothing. You would imagine how good it feels to feel healthier. You would imagine looking like your ideal body weight.

If I said to you, "Imagine helping 1 billion people every day in their personal lives," what would that look like to you? You could absolutely imagine creating a way for people to become healthier or creating a newer technology. There is limitless ways to help 1 billion people.

If I said to you, "Imagine buying your dream house with the most perfect view," you would absolutely be able to look out the back or front and see the breath taking view. You would be able to imagine having your friends and family come over to enjoy the view with you.

If it enters the mind, it is possible. Impossible is only an idea and ideas are not always true or relevant. You give meaning to everything in your life. Everything is possible. Give the word "impossible" zero meaning and that is what your reality will become. With vision, understand the culture that you want to create. Culture is everything. When you create a vision with bad culture, the vision will be bad. When you create a vision with good culture, the vision will be good. Culture is the people, their social behaviors, and the norms within the culture.

People will not care about your vision. That is the sad reality. We all put our own interests first and we like to talk about ourselves. You and only you are going to have to believe in your vision. If your vision is powerful enough and you are making progress, successful people will get on board and unsuccessful people will not want to help.

When you create and act on your vision, make sure it is out of love. Do what you love with like-minded people. If people are like you, they will want to help you bring your vision into existence. Ideally, your vision is something that you love so much that the work that you do feels like playing. Doing something only for the money will never sustain. If your why and the foundational belief is just money, it will not be a very purposeful vision. When you vision beyond money, money will follow. Money does not lead, money only follows.

What you fear will appear and what you look at will disappear. You cannot beat Mother Nature and your vision will require a lot of patience. Anything worth doing is going to require a lot of patience. If you are not patient, you will have already lost. Like Black and White, you need to find the Balance in your vision. The mathematical laws of life can all be Balanced. A problem is Balanced by the solution. Like time, you can live in a different time zone in your same region. Your vision may be real, but not yet.

Life is constantly changing and the changes of life may alter your vision. Even if you paid for something, it is not yours. If you own something, it is not yours. Life evolves at any moment in time and it may take anything away from you to make future growth possible. Do not be attached to anything physical because it can be gone in a heartbeat. Life happens when you are living. Visions can go side ways, but it is up to you to adjust your visions. Laws of nature and life are forever and always changing. Nature and life always have plans and are not anticipated so easily. Nothing is forever and everything is going to change sooner or later. Life is very multidimensional.

When you are happy, you are in a different dimension than when you are sad. When you feel selfish, you are in a different dimension than when you are selfless. Emotion is very multidimensional and sometimes you need to ponder what dimension of emotion you are in. If you can master your emotional dimensions and alter your dimensions to more desired dimensions during moments, you will be able to thrive in life. Emotion and change are going to be the two biggest factors for you to develop a higher quality of life for yourself.

If you do not like something or if you hate something, change it. Change things that are not evolving you or making you happy. If your friend is bringing you down and you feel that they are not worth your time anymore, change your friend. If your career is making you miserable and you feel a loss of energy, change your career. If you do not like your routine, change your routine. If you do not like where you are living, change your location. If you do not like where you are learning, change your school. If you do not like the clothes that you are wearing, change your wardrobe. If you do not like the gym that you are going to, change your gym. If you do not like the way your room looks, change the layout. If you do not like negativity, change your attitude. You can change everything. If you do not like everything, change everything.

You have conscious choices and your decisions can be made by conscious actions. Look and you will find anything. Do not look and you may also find, but do not optimize on the exceptions. Every decision that we make is based on our emotional state. Every decision is an emotional decision. We give meaning based on our emotion. Something may mean a lot if our emotions Balance accordingly. Something may mean very little if our emotions do not Balance accordingly.

Passion and commitment is key to make visions a reality. Followed by relentlessly working towards the vision. Make your vision of great value. To provide great value, you have to give it your all.

I understand that you are going to be emotional. Even I want to feel sadness sometimes. I am not saying that you need to become a robot, but what I am saying is to master your emotions. When your emotions are in check during emotional moments, you will be able to progress towards your goals in life in a very productive way.

Your vision cannot be great if you do not love it. If you still do not believe in your vision, I want you to put this book down and go take a walk. Walk around your block. Walk to the nearest park, restaurant, store, and then come back to this book. If you come back to this book, you just proved that one step at a time will get you there. Do not continue reading this book until you have walked to a location and back. Prove to yourself that one step at a time will get you to your vision. Vision that park near your house and walk there. When you walk and see the park, you will have fulfilled your vision. Your vision follows the same blue print. Maybe you will not see the park right away in your vision, but I promise you that if you take one step at a time, you will get to the park somehow, someway.

Time does not need to feel like it is dragging on. You can be on your purpose and on the natural course of your life towards your vision and greatest dreams. It is just going to require some work on your part. Time will tell. If you do not have a vision, work on creating one. Visions are based on your values and the things that you love. It only takes work. Visions are achieved by continuously exhausting all angles until your vision is achieved. It may take one or many angles to achieve a vision. If you can think it, you can achieve it. It only takes the right angle or angles once to complete the vision. You do not have to do it again once you complete the vision. You only have to get it right once.

Be observant in the world. See things that others do not see. Bounce ideas off a close friend. Get the idea juices flowing. You can tell the difference between a successful person and a non-successful person based on how they handle failure. Successful people learn a lesson, unsuccessful people blame. Successful people will get up and unsuccessful people stay down. To create a vision is easy, but to execute that vision is hard. It is going to take everything that you have got to breathe your vision into life. It is going to take your mind, body, emotions, and soul to complete your greatest vision.

How do you want to live? Ask yourself the question and think of the answer. If you could live exactly the way that you wanted, what would that look like to you? How you live is a result of the things that you do. The majority of your life will be spent at your work or on your business. The job that you spend so much of your time on is going to dictate your life to a great degree. You are going to be doing things in your personal life based on your professional life. Your job dictates your socioeconomic status which influences where you go, what you do, and how you live to a great extent. Your job influences what kind of relationships that you have, because the people that you work with are going to be the people that you spend the most time with. Your work will factor in certain stresses to your life that can hurt your health and make you not want to take care of yourself or your health. Your job is very important in determining the quality of your life. You are a representation of the value that you contribute in your job.

Many people have chosen a profession completely randomly and it may not be something that they love or are passionate about. Most people take a job because it was convenient to be employed at the time. People underestimate the power of their job's effect on their mind. Your job molds how you think and what you do. What you do is what makes your life yours. Sooner or later, you are going to need to dance with reality and think about how your job is affecting you. Is your job making you feel that you are progressing towards your vision? Or is your job making you feel that you are not progressing towards your vision?

You are going to become what you focus on and you are what you do repeatedly. Your thoughts become your words and your words have a great potential to become your actions. Some actions are great and some actions are not so great. Through the completion of your vision, you may need to reinvent yourself. It is not what you do, but how you live. No matter what you do, live it authentically and be true to yourself. Focus on where it is that you are going to be in the future. Once you know where you are going to be in the future, focus on where you are going to be after your future becomes your present. What we do is what is in our mind. Your vision is the compass to your dreams.

Think outside of the box. Lose your mind. No vision has been great without a hint of craziness. Crazy people change the world. Think big and think crazy. Crazy can become not crazy and not crazy can become crazy. Never care if people agree or disagree with you or your vision. In the end, your happiness is the only thing that matters. If you are only making others happy and yourself miserable, you are missing the key element of Balance. Make yourself happy and the world will become happy. Allow yourself to find new truths and new meanings in your vision that you did not realize before. Life evolves because it wants things to become better. Bettering ourselves is part of our nature.

Like time, everything is moving forward and not back. Things are becoming better and not worse. When you work on bettering yourself, Mother Nature will want to evolve you because you are acting in accordance to the law of nature. When you do not help yourself to develop, you are going against nature and nature will eventually make you pay. It is called Mother Nature because mothers want to raise us to grow and become stronger. Do not make Mother Nature mad by not doing anything.

How do you want to live? What emotions do you want to feel and be present? Emotions tell us how we feel about how we live our life. Most people would agree that they want happy emotions to be present in their lives. People would want positive emotions present in their lives. You should focus on the things that make you happy to make happiness arise in your life.

I want to live richer and to feel more secure
I want to live healthier and to feel better about myself
I want to live in a happier world and to feel calmer

I want to live loving everything and everyone and to feel love
I want to live in peace and to feel relaxed
I want to live doing the things that I love and to feel fulfilled
I want to live in a healthy romantic relationship and to feel
appreciated
I want to live in a world where I am able to help billions of people
to feel a difference
I want to live giving my talents to feel a sense of purpose
I want to live in forgiveness and to feel free
I want to live traveling and to feel curiosity

Think about how you want to live and what you want to feel
and write your thoughts on a notepad. Write down everything
that you envision and you will feel better. When you write down
your emotional state, you will not have to feel it so much because
you are now aware of your feelings. To cry is a delicate thing of
beauty, crying is strength. Cry if you have to get something out
of your system. Do not fear crying. We have been conditioned
to believe that crying is weakness and that is untrue. If you care
about something, it will bring tears to your eyes.

When you write down your vision for your eyes and mind to
see, you reinforce the idea that your dreams are achievable and
that you will make them come into reality. Visions are reality
before reality has happened. How do you want to impact others?
How do you want to impact your children? How do you want to
impact the public?

Create the momentum and inspiration deep down to the core of
your heart. Hang up a picture of the person or thing that inspires
you and that you are fighting for, even if it is a picture of you.

Create forces to make your visions and greatest dreams happen.
The forces come forward through your habits, your thoughts,
and your beliefs. Think before you act. Never act before you
think and do not think for too long. Do not think for too long,
act indefinitely until your vision is reached. What we think is
what we put in our minds. Your mind is a universe within itself.

Do not spread negativity in your mind's universe. Only spread positivity in your mind's universe. Imagination is the key to creating a bright vision.

Imagine running through a cemetery and falling into a bottomless pit right into your grave. Imagine never being able to get out of the bottomless pit and you are dead forever. Imagine if you did not complete your vision and dreams. Imagine the immense pain that you would feel. Think about the shame and the remorse. You are not invincible and your clock is ticking every moment. Your life could abruptly end in 30 seconds from now no matter who you are. Chase your vision. Go to the graveyard forever having completed all of your greatest visions. Be in your grave having lived a purposeful life. Do not bring your dreams and visions to the grave with you.

Go to a cemetery because it is the richest place in the entire world. It is the richest place in the world because a lot of people that are not here today have taken their dreams to the cemetery that you are at. Read the tombstones of the people that left this world and see when they were born and when they had passed. You will realize that life is very short and your time is very limited. Time is scarce and it is your most valuable commodity. Time is greater than your health. Even if you do not have any health left, time will be your last essence.

You can do a lot in a little time
You can do little in a lot of time
You can do a lot in a lot of time
You can do little in a little time

You get to choose how you want your reality to be. Every choice is yours. You can live your vision or you can pass on your vision. You can work on your vision or not work on your vision. The choice is consciously yours. You need to have a heart to heart conversation with yourself about your vision and how you are going to get to the end.

Guard your vision from external poison and create the anti-poison to protect your mind from negativity. The difference between animals in the wild and humans is that humans have an imagination and animals do not. Humans are the only animals with imagination. This indicates that imagination is part of your purpose. Imagination allows you to see your dreams before it actually happens. See what it would look like 10 years from now, 15 years from now, 20 years from now, or 25 years from now. Imagine becoming that person who you were meant to be. Do it because you want to, not because you have to. You should innately do the things that you want to. You should innately want to act on your vision if you love it.

Block the world out and focus on your vision. Forget about everything around you. Do not use the present as an excuse to not live in the future. To become great, sacrifice what you are now for what you can become later. To become great, you need to overcome a great obstacle. No one great has ever become great without overcoming a major obstacle or obstacles. Live in your future, see your future, see what you are going to become and be. See yourself there before it happens.

Do not focus on the pain in your imagination. Pain is inevitable but focus on the end goal. You may not see success now, but success may see you. Success needs to see you before you can see it. One day will be your time to shine. If you quit, you will never see the day of your future vision. Failure does not push you back. Failure only pushes you forward towards your success. Keep your imagination and vision strong even through hardship and failures. When someone exhausts action persistently without stopping, failure eventually gives up and success sustains. To help your vision become realized, get out of your bubble and take risks. If there are no risks, there are no rewards. In life, the greater the risk, the greater the reward. It is mathematically logical. Think about your dream clearly until you are able to walk into your new life.

Wake up and live your vision. Focus on nothing except for your vision. Forget about what is going on around you no matter how bad that it may be. Your vision is a reality and you need to live that reality until your vision is no longer a vision but a physical reality in real time. Forget about falling back on something. Focus on your greatest vision because your secondary fall back vision is not going to be as great as your biggest vision. If you focus on your fall back secondary vision, it will not help you to hyper focus on your primary vision. You will not be as happy living your secondary vision as you will be living your primary vision. Never settle. Go for the best and forget the rest. Your initial vision is the best and truest form of yourself and that is worth going after.

When you live your vision in reality, your emotions will become heightened and you will feel emotions more intensely. You will become emotional when you are at the place of your dream. You will feel emotional because you will think about how your vision was a tiny thought that occurred in your mind and grew to such a large scale. A thought became reality because you put in the work to make it come into existence. It will uplift your spirits. When you get to the place of your dreams, nothing will get in your way because you will have already climbed the biggest mountain in your life. Completing your primary vision gives you the momentum to complete bigger and greater things in the course of your life. Life is all about momentum building. When the ball rolls fast enough, it will not stop.

You cannot do anything without believing in the end product of your vision. Nobody will believe until you believe. When you invest in yourself, others will invest in you. If you do not believe in yourself, who is going to believe in you? Believing is the engine that will get you to the end of your vision. Reinforce your belief during your journey and keep telling yourself that you believe in what you are doing. If you your belief is strong, you will get to your desired vision. Bring your vision out through your DNA that you were given. Ignite the bomb of your vision and life that you planted and it will explode. When the bomb explodes, it will create a great supernova and that supernova will transform you into a big superstar.

Black and White Balance is all about the transformation of light through a place of great darkness into the brightest light source. You must go through the darkness to get to the light at the end of the tunnel. Every vision that you create is a tunnel. All you can see is the light at the end but you cannot see what is in the tunnel. If you could see what is in the tunnel, you would not learn anything. If you did not learn anything through your failures, what would be the point of your success? You are going to undergo a lot of disappointment and unease before your vision is realized and you will be made when you overcome the disappointments. When things are uneasy and filled with tension, that force is what is trying to evolve you into the greater ease and resolution. Tension eventually releases, but you cannot have a release without tension present first. Do not allow hardship to rob you of your dreams. Your dreams are waiting for you. Your vision is the insight to see where your dreams lie. You need to see before you can see.

There is no such thing as a special few people capable of realizing their dreams. Everybody was born with the potential to live his or her dream. It universally exists in all of us. You were born to do more than pay bills and live a mediocre life before you leave this universe and dimension. You were created for extraordinary. Everybody was born to live his or her dreams. The only problem is that people complain, but do not do anything about their situation. Complaining is just excuses and sheer laziness. Always work on yourself and exercise your vision.

Fear of failing is the worst excuse that we tell ourselves. The reason is because without failure, you will never become greatly successful. Nobody became greatly successful overnight without failure. Failure is the recipe for success. If you are giving something all you have and you are failing, that means that you are growing and succeeding. Pain and being uncomfortable create the more evolved success. Success is the byproduct of high numbers of failures. The greater the number of failures, the greater the end success will be. The fear of success is the second worst excuse that we tell ourselves. The reason is because if you are living out your calling that you were designed to do, you will not care about what anybody thinks because you will be immensely happy and fulfilled. Pleasing people should be taken out of your vocabulary. Who cares what people think about you and who cares if you fail in front of people. They are your failures, not anybody else's. Life goes on.

People may laugh, but deep down they really do not care about your failures. If people that barely know you really care about your failures, then their life is really sad. They should focus on themselves as you should focus on yourself. Stop learning about other people more than you know yourself. Start learning about yourself. Who cares if people do not like you? Many people sadly know more about someone else's life than they care to learn about their life. Become the right person for your vision. When you focus on your vision, your life takes on a whole greater meaning. The greater meaning becomes a more purposeful meaning. Do not be a copycat, be your own cat.

Align every element of your life with your vision to make your vision a reality. Invest and double down on yourself to make your visions real. Invest in your time and be alone for a while. The most successful people disappear for a while and then surprise everybody when they come back. To give you an example, writing this book is very lonely. I enjoy the loneliness and the peace that I have with my own thoughts and ideas. My vision while writing this book is to finish writing the book so that I can bring the value of this book to you. The end goal of my vision is to enrich your life with knowledge and wisdom to help you live a better life. I want your life to be the very best that it can be. I want you to see it within yourself that you are worth it and can have anything that your heart desires. It can all change for you if you change it. You and only you, no one else is going to do the work for you. Like my vision with this book, your vision can be achieved too. No matter how big or how small that your vision may be.

You can touch millions of people's lives if you are ambitious enough in your vision. You can make your family proud, your friends proud, your community proud, your children proud, your spouse proud, and you can make yourself proud. Whoever it is that you want to make proud, you can achieve it by working excruciatingly hard on your vision. Everybody wants things to happen, but not everybody is willing to go through with the hard work that comes along with making something happen. Tell yourself that it is not over until you win. Winning is the only option that you have, there is no such thing as losing. No matter the outcome, if you never give up, you will always be a winner. Starting a vision is hard, working on the vision is the hardest, and finishing the vision is the easiest. Starting is always hard, but once you start and you create momentum, it only becomes easier. The only person that can start your vision is you. The greatest symbolism for your vision is a mirror. Take a closer look in the mirror. You will see your vision. Visions are only a mindset. You must act on the mindset. Execution happens all day and every day. You have the power to make your visual hallucinations come into existence. The best practice that you can do for your self is to look at yourself in a mirror. Imagine what your vision and dream would look like. Once you see your dream, imagine running and jumping into the mirror and landing into the mirror dream. What if that could be your reality when you complete your vision?

If you love it, you will be willing to suffer for it. Visions take some time, the bigger the vision, the longer that it will take. I promise you that if you put in the time to achieve your vision, it will be worth all of your efforts and suffering. The emotional experience that you will feel will be absolutely divine. Your spirit will lift to a height that it has never been lifted to. Butterflies will flutter throughout your stomach and the emotional stimulation will be euphoric. You will feel out of this universe and you will feel that you will be able to conquer anything because you will be able to conquer anything. The most mystical feeling is envisioning something in your mind and then to be living it. Imagine living your dream and your dream is what is living.

Chills occur, the little hairs on the back of your neck will stand up. Your heart will drop in warmth when other people see your new evolved self. Your eyes will twinkle like the stars above. You may feel light headed and you will feel nervous because you are not used to living your dream. Living your dream is like meeting the love of your life for the first time. The burning lust when you see the person for the first time is going to feel the exact same way when you finally get to that place of your dream. When you wake up, it will not even feel real. You may stay up late in disbelief that your dream is here and that you are living it. It is the single greatest reward in the world to be living out your dream. The only thing between you and your dream is work and time. When you get to your dream, you may be terrified. The fear will pass. You earned it, you made it. You have everything that you want. You carried out your vision and now it is here. Everything is so much better when you are living your dream. Every moment suddenly becomes magical. Everything seems to go perfect when you are living out dreams. Paradise in this universe has enchanted you.

You are now living out your dream and most people can only dream of living the quality of life that you are now living. Most people in life do not live out their dreams. You are doing something that few people get to experience. Everyone wants to live out their dreams, but not everyone gets to live out their dreams. People get in the way of themselves. When you are living out your dream, you feel the need to give more. You want to become a better person when you are that happy and that fulfilled. Success breeds success. Now that you are successful, you want to help others to become successful just like you are. You will think differently, you will feel differently, and most importantly, you will live differently. Life will never be the same.

When your time is up and you must leave this world, you can go to the grave fulfilled and feel that you have lived a purposeful life. When you are living your dream, you are only doing the thing that you are most passionate about and the thing that you love. You no longer have to work because work feels like play. Time flies when you are having fun and enjoying yourself and time goes slow when you are not having fun or enjoying yourself. You only have to execute to achieve your dream once and then it is yours. That is, until you create a different dream to pursue. If you can achieve a dream once, you can achieve a dream again.

The best way to achieve a dream is to skillfully become a master of something. Too many people dabble in too many things. When you put your focus on one thing to master, you will achieve it. It is better to be extraordinary at one thing than average at two things. Quality always beats quantity. When you become a master at something better than anybody else at a particular thing, you become valuable. When you are valuable, your life becomes more valuable. When your life becomes more valuable, you will attract more valuable people into your life. To live a valuable life is to live a higher quality life. Achieve mastery in one thing, the thing that you love most. High value attracts high value and low value attracts low value.

It is going to take a great amount of sacrifice to achieve your dream. The best thing that you can do is to follow your heart's desires because it will lead you to a happier state of mind. When you become happy doing the thing that you love most, that is what it means to be living out your purpose. Do not do things that you hate, unless they will help you to get to your dream. When the road is ugly, the end will be beautiful. The greater the ugliness that is on your road, the more beautiful the end of the road will be. Great ugliness is Balanced by great beauty.

Your dream is calling you through your vision and it is waiting for you to see it before you see it. Now it is time to execute your vision. When you finally do get to the place of your dream, you will experience the greatest fulfillment that you will ever know.

It is time for you to go to your dream.

8

Money

We live with a cursed force that has caused great happiness, misery, bloodshed, and wars. It is something that impacts us directly and indirectly every day. It is the main conversation shared in social settings amongst people. It is taboo, almost humorous. There are so many interpretations and beliefs about it. The cursed force is money.

Money is the medium by which one measures worldly success. People measure someone's value by their net worth and their bank account. People treat people differently when someone has money compared to someone that does not have money. We live in a capitalist society. In a capitalist society, anyone can get rich. Fame is usually associated with fortune, but fame and fortune will not bring you happiness. Money is not everything.

Money is highly important and it is necessary to make. Many people have false beliefs about money. Money is a tool. Money is nothing more than a tool. If you use the tool effectively, it can bring your dreams into reality. The more money that you have, the more control you can have. Time is money and money is time. When you have money, you can live how you want to. The unfortunate reality is if you have money, people will take what you have to say more seriously. Of course, you can make a positive impact without money, but money will make it much easier. When you have proven yourself in business, people are more inclined to listen to you. People do not want to see reality the way that it is.

Suffering will always come to you when you want reality to be other than it is. You can ignore reality, but the consequences of reality will still take place. Accept money and look at money positively. Money can be used for good or it can be used for bad. Money can be good and money can be bad. Money exposes what kind of person you are. The more abundance of wealth that you have, the more exposed that you will be. How you spend your money is a great mirror of the person that you are. You should spend your money on the things that you believe in.

Money will help bring you more stability in your life, if used properly. Stability makes your mental and emotional state calmer. Calmness is essential for a successful life. Most people do not understand the laws of money. The laws of money are highly mathematical. Economics and finance are a mathematical science that is extremely important. The game of money has rules. Money is a game. Business is a mind game. If you want to reach mastery of yourself and success, financial literacy is unquestionably the thing that is going to shape you to be successful of your overall life.

Physically fit shape to control your health
Emotionally control yourself and how you respond to things
Relationships to control network and have love
Financial awareness to control stability and resources
Energy levels to control your motivation
Certainty to control your beliefs
Time to control outcomes

The above seven are the things a person must be adept at to be overall successful. The acronym above spells PERFECT. Of course, nothing is perfect. Perfect is an imperfection and imperfection is perfect. Take control of your life or it will take control of you. When you master financial literacy and you have money, it will become a lot easier to manage your overall success. Money is not everything, but it sure helps. Money cannot buy total health, bring the dead back to life, increase time beyond your time, or many other things.

Money can buy better nutrition and health products
Money can buy things that increase your emotional state to a more
 positive one
Money can take financial stress away and make it easier to focus
 on relationships
Money can buy more time for yourself to live your life how you
 want to live

Time to talk about the mathematical laws and rules about money. You will see why there is becoming a greater gap between the rich and the poor. The middle class is disappearing. Things always go up and they never go down. Things go down momentarily, but the cost of living is always increasing.

The reasons for poverty and the extreme lack of material possessions and money is: Lack of access to education, limited access to credit, inherited poverty, discrimination, social inequality, physical or mental disabilities, mental illness, health issues, war, violence, crime, politics, corruption, overpopulation, unemployment, overpricing of food and other basic needs, low income, insufficient benefits, unsanitary conditions, epidemic diseases, hunger, slavery, military conquest, history, debt, natural disasters, lack of resources, riots and protests, religion, lack of family support, lack of planning, addiction, financial illiteracy, poverty mindset, overspending, and restrictions of options.

Those are not all of the reasons why people are in great poverty or debt. There are countless more reasons. Maybe this opens your eyes to all of the reasons that you may have scarcity in your life. Most people in the course of their life are going to experience financial hardship or limited spending power. Most people also experience debt in their life. If you are reading this and you are in great debt, I promise you that things are going to get better for you. You can get rid of the debt. Money is a game and a mindset.

Once you recognize why you have debt or why you are broke, you can recover. When you find the problem, you can become solution based. Every problem has a solution. Things do not happen overnight, but things can happen a lot quicker for you than you may think. There are a lot of reasons why you may have a lack of money, but the good news is that there are a lot of ways to make money. There are virtually infinite ways to make money. First define what becoming rich or richer looks like to you. Understand that wealth is abundance of valuable resources and possessions.

The ways that people make money and become richer are: Use of science, education, reading, taking action, learning from financial mentors that are more affluent than them, change in lifestyle, saving, selling a product or service that is physical or virtual, promotion, freelancing, coaching, training, consulting, speaking, events, design, donations, networking, premium content, marketing, ads, following a passion, downgrading their car, sell items online, tutoring, catering and cooking, photography, modeling, recycling, cleaning, part-time side jobs, social media, video blogs, acting, developing, being creative, investing, stock market, crypto currency, real estate, taking risks, personal branding, collaborating with someone that has a bigger audience, Amazon, eBay, starting a business, living frugally, inheritance or lottery, solving problems, selling a business, creating passive income, write-offs, precious resources.

The above ways mentioned to make money is not even a fraction of 1% of all of the ways that you can make money. There are infinite ways to promote wealth creation. It takes minor creativity and research to create a more financially abundant life for you to live. Go to the library and read books on wealth creation or go online to learn. It is a lot easier to make money and create wealth for yourself if you become solution based.

Time to talk about the mathematical laws and rules of money.

The most important law that people fail to accept is that:

1. Money is a game and the game is money.

Money is a game and the way to win the game is to play the game. In the game of money, the more that you play the game and the more that you learn about the game, the better at the game that you will be.

Higher earners are winning the game. I know that it does not sound fair, but life is not fair. Life is not fair and fair is not life. Life is fairly unfair and unfairly fair. If you can accept and understand that people that are currently making more money than you are playing the game better than you, it may give you the inspiration to play the game better too. Just because someone else is winning the game, does not mean that you cannot win the game too. Everyone on this planet is playing the same game. The best way to play the game is to learn and become best friends with money. If you learn more about your friend money, then money and you will have a closer relationship with each other. Money will want to see you if you take an interest in it. There is a reason that people say that you are either earning interest or paying interest. You must be interested in money. If you do not care about money, money will not care about you.

The more you learn and play, the more money will come your way. Money is a game and if you learn the science of the game, you will be making lots of money. The key element to playing the game and one of the best approaches in life is to be in a state of non-attachment. Being attached to an outcome takes an enormous amount of energy during and after the efforts. Long after you fail, you will still feel the pain of your attachment to the outcome. Something magical happens when you focus on doing something in the moment. If you fail, just adjust for next time. Outcomes are going to occur whenever actions are taken. When you are non-attached, you enjoy the process and have fun with it. The process is everything.

In fact, attachment creates fear. The reason that people fail is because their attachment to an outcome creates a fear of loss if the desired outcome is not achieved. When the fear of loss is present, it starts pushing the thing that you are trying to achieve away from you. Fear repels things and non-attachment attracts things. It is the North and South law of magnetic force that creates this phenomenon. North magnet attracts South magnet. North magnet repels North magnet and South magnet repels South magnet. Your non-attachment will create the force for your desired outcome to have an attachment to you and you will attract it. Success is the overcoming of failures and progress always involves risk. If you care enough, you will be persistent and get over the failure obstacles and succeed. When you are non-attached, you win whether something works out or does not work out.

The next law is that:

2. Money is a doubles game and the game doubles.
Money doubles positively and it also doubles negatively
$1,000
$2,000
$4,000
$8,000
$16,000
$32,000
$64,000
$128,000
$256,000
$512,000
$1,024,000
$2,048,000
$4,096,000
$8,192,000
$16,384,000
$32,768,000
$65,536,000
$131,072,000
$262,144,000
$524,288,000
$1,048,576,000

Above is doubled from one thousand (1,000) to past one billion (1,000,000,000).

You are currently looking at the doubling process to making a billion dollars. To get to 1 billion dollars, you need to double from $1,000 20 times. The fact that you are able to do the math proves that you have limitless capability to achieve anything that your heart desires. Everything comes down to math and numbers. If you want anything in life, it is only mathematical.

The numbers go up in doubles and respectively the numbers go into the negative doubles past zero. Figure out how you can double from $1,000 to $2,000 and you will have doubled your money. If you make $1,000 a 1000 times, you will have made one million dollars (1,000,000).

If you have $4,000 and you are spending your money, the law of money will be trying to push you down to $2,000. Money pushes downwards in doubles. Although money rises slowly, falls happen fast. Making money takes longer than spending money. Money can fall beyond doubles, but only raises in doubles. However, generally speaking, it raises and falls in doubles unless extreme earning or spending occurs. It does not matter what your number is. If your number is $3,387, then try to find a way to double it to $6,774. If your number is $100, then try to find a way to double it to $200.

Focus on your double game, not on someone else's double game. The game of money works in leagues and some leagues you cannot even compete in. If someone's double game is doubling from $10,000,000 to $20,000,000 and you are doubling from $50,000 to $100,000, they are playing in a different ballpark than you. If you try and compete with someone that is of much higher doubles than you are, you may make a reckless decision and financially suffer greatly.

The best way to control and focus on your game is to live within your means. The goal is to gain doubles and not to lose doubles. Do no be extravagant if you cannot afford it and do not make dicey investments if you do not know what you are doing. If you comfortably have the means to buy something, then it will not matter. It only matters when you cannot afford something. If you are spending and do not have at least double the money in the bank of what you are spending your money on, do not buy it. 1 to 5, 5 to 10, 10 to 20, 20 to 50, 50 to 100. Think about the intervals of currency. Your money is a tool and works best in doubles. Money is perspective and ratios.

Some people can afford to spend $90,000 in one night at a nightclub and some people can only afford to spend $10 in one night at a nightclub. It is just different ratios of the same doubles game of money. The money game is the same game, just different levels of the game.

The next law is that:

3. Money is a spiritual force and a spiritual force is money.
Money does not like negative people
Money does not like desperate people
Money likes people who are non-attached
Money likes people who solve problems
Money likes people who are stable
Money likes people with good judgment
Money can help your life or ruin your life
Money is emotionless
Money is unforgiving
Money gets bored and does not like being in one place for too long
Money needs to move and it leaves if it is bored
Money is genderless
Money is not a leader, but a follower
Money follows attention and movement
Money can control your life
Money can be used for good or for evil
Money is earned through level of value provided
Money creates change
Money is physical and non-physical
Money is a distant relative of karma
Money favors some people over others naturally
Money grows money and lack of money diminishes money

Money does not care about your feelings or how good of a person
    that you are
Money is measurable
Money can buy most things, but it cannot buy everything
Money and emotion do not mix

The best approach to earning more money is to be non-attached
to money directly and do what you love. Money is a byproduct of
you doing the thing that you love most. Money will come to you
when you do what you love because you are not focused on the
soul outcome of money. Money does not like desperation. When
you do something just for the money and there is no attachment
to love, money will be limited. Money is attracted to love. When
you are focusing your attention on something that you love, money
will follow that attention. If you focus only on the money, you
will give up too easily.

There are more laws about money and you will find out the
laws as you play and learn more about the game. Every rule and
law always has an exception. Even universal laws may have an
exception. Do not optimize on the exception, optimize on the
general rule. The general rule is the best standard to follow in most
cases. Some laws change and some laws do not change. There is
more than one way to be educated and there is more than one
way to make money.

The next rule of money is:

4. Study your local politicians and people making money.
The laws where you live are created and put into place by politicians. Politicians are human beings and human beings are not
always perfect or work in the best interest of the public. Politicians
create financial laws. You need to understand your local politician's
philosophies and what they are going to do. The politicians may
heavily increase taxes or they may lower taxes. They may offer
better tax incentives. Your politicians influence your environment
and economy around you. People are becoming very closed minded

especially the young people in society. They think that their vote will not make a difference and that all politicians are corrupt. That is simply untrue. Your vote counts 100% and has influence. Especially in local politics, your vote will make a lot more of a difference. You need to take charge of your life and pay attention to the leaders of your area. If you neglect to follow politics, your financial standings can take a serious dive and leave you vulnerable. You have a right to vote and to be informed by the positions that your leaders take a stand on.

Government can increase taxes on roads, public transportation, education, sanitation, legal systems, public safety, research, public insurance, health-care, pensions, unemployment benefits, energy, water, waste management, gas prices, income taxes, capital gains, corporate taxes, property taxes, inheritance, expatriation, goods and services, sales taxes, meat taxes, environmental taxes, direct and indirect taxes, fees, cigarettes, liquor.

There are more taxes than I can possibly name. Some taxes may affect more people than others, some taxes may not affect some people, and some taxes can be detrimental to a person's financial standings. Imagine if ten heavy-duty taxes were suddenly introduced into your economy, that could seriously set you back financially. If you do not understand the taxes imposed and implemented by government officials, you have a great potential to fall behind quickly. At the end of the day, the government and politicians are going to do what is in their best interest because they are a business. Any business operates in the best interest of the company and the people that run the business. There are good politicians and there are bad politicians. Protect yourself financially by arming yourself with knowledge about the politicians in your community. If people do not question and understand their politician's philosophies, fascism and tyrannical governance can result. It is an extreme case, but it happened during World War II. History can repeat itself. When people learn critical thinking and question the practices of government and their agencies, the misuse of power will be limited. Higher taxes and less favorable economic shifts can happen if you are ignorant and do not take the time to study basic politics. Lastly, you may be losing money unknowingly if you do not comprehend how certain taxes work or learn about new taxes that are implemented.

You do not have to master politics, but an above basic understanding of political viewpoints will help you greatly in mastering your financial prosperity. Your government creates the laws of money in your economy and that is highly important knowledge to comprehend. Many people neglect politics and think that it is cool to not know and to not care. In the end, they pay. Learn and adjust to achieve financial increase and proficiency. Govern your own money or someone else will. You are the representative of your bank account and it is for you to do a good job representing your money. After all, money is the blood of business and there are a lot of parasites ready to suck the blood from you. The richer you get, the easier it gets. The government is going to be the biggest parasite of your life. It has been said that the only two things guaranteed in life are death and taxes.

Remember that it is nothing personal, just business. When you are poor, it is a lot harder, but not impossible. When you are a business owner, you will receive plenty of tax breaks. Natural selection takes place. People that are rich are naturally selected to live. When you are poor, you are trying to be killed off by natural selection. It is survival of the fittest. The richest are the fittest. I know that you may feel mad hearing that, but it is reality. Do not let that discourage you because you can be the exception to the rule that works hard and pulls yourself from poor to middle class and from middle class to rich.

Part two of this rule is to study people making money. You become whom you surround yourself with. When you see the way that successful people think and study their thought processes, you learn why they are the way they are. You become what you think. If a successful person thinks a certain way and you see how they think, it would be wise to copy the way that they think. Not everything is going to work for you. What works for someone may not work for you. Borrow thought processes from successful people and make them your own to potentially live differently.

It is a good idea to hang out with a richer person compared to a poorer person because then you will be able to see a difference in mindset and mentality. Financially successful and financially unsuccessful people think differently. The proof is in the pudding because suppose that you take someone that is completely rich and you take all of their money away. With due time, they will become rich again because of the way that they think. Poor people remain the same unless their thought process changes. It is so important to get people into your circle that are far more developed than you in a particular field, whether it be finance, skill, wisdom, spirituality, talent, or anything that you aspire to be. What you aspire to be, will be, if you position yourself to win. Yes, you can strategically position yourself to win or to be in a more favorable position to win. What a master could teach you in a short time is much greater than what an amateur could teach you in a long time. It will always be quality over quantity. Get quality people that can pull you up rather than pull you down. Rich people will make you richer and poor people will make you poorer. It is common nature. Like attracts like. In anything you do, command the best people into your life. Get the best business partners that you can find. Get the best and forget the rest. If you get less than adequate, you will suffer in learning. Learn from the great producers. The rule of business is that the more money that you produce for people, the more that they will do business with you.

The next rule of money is:

5. You must make progress and progress must be made.
You need crystal clear clarity in your vision. You cannot have a clear vision if you are not actively making progress towards something better. It does not matter how fast or how slow you are making progress as long as you are making progress. Go as slow as you have to if that means going forward.

The best way to make progress in the financial world is to actively beat your financial goals. If you are a start up business and you made $1,000 in your first month, of course you can think in doubles and aim at $2,000. Ideally that would be the best, but if you beat $1,000 by $100 for the sum of $1,100 then you will have beat your previous month. Beat your previous month, quarterly, semi, annually, 5 year, and 10 year, whatever it may be. If you made $1,000 in your first month, you can aim to make $1,200-$1,500 the next month. Again, it does not matter how fast that you go, as long as you are making progress forward.

Develop your talents and learn. When you grow, your bank account grows. Your bank account is a mirror of how great that you are playing the game of money. Your bank account is a scorecard. When your score is high in the game, what that means is that you are doing well at the game. Progress the numbers upwards, not downwards. Save and conserve, do not be wasteful with your money. Respect money. If you have credit card debt, focus only on paying off the debt. Forget about wasting your money on high-end coffee shops and other miscellaneous small luxuries until the debt is zero. $10 spent could be $10 towards paying off your debt. If you are paying your credit card debt off, you are getting richer. You are going up and not down. Every dollar counts no matter how big that your debt may be. You are not losing money by investing your money towards escaping your debt. When you make large purchases or frequent small purchases on things that you do not need, you are only robbing yourself and delaying your progress. To think that today, you could eliminate going to high-end coffee shops every morning and live your life only through bare necessities. It does not cost as much to live as you think that it does, if you live only to satisfy your basic needs. Today, you could make your own coffee and save a fortune over a year. Do what you need to do to make progress. When you save money, you are making progress. When you stop wanting things, the things that you want will want you. Focus on your needs and Balance the wants purposefully and strategically. People delay their progress by spending more on their wants than spending on only the things that they need.

You could get ahead today by selling things that you no longer need. Sell something that you love and toughen up. Make yourself progress. If something in your company is costing you too much and is not giving you a good return on your investment (ROI), then it is time to get rid of it. Sell it. You can increase your money and progress right now. If a car is costing you too much, downgrade. You are in control of your progress a lot more than you think. You are responsible for your financial future. The future is now.

Being with people better than you will make your progression surge quickly forward. There are many ways to speed up your progress if you just become a little bit creative. It takes minor creativity to progress. Become solution based. Keep beating your financial goals every time. If you do not beat your financial goal, work twice as hard the next month to beat the previous goal. It just takes energy and dedication to get ahead.

Ask yourself, "Am I making progress by beating my financial goals?" Or "Am I not making progress by beating my financial goals?" It is going to be either one or the other, so adjust accordingly. Make a strategy and decide how you are going to beat your next financial goal. The more goals you beat, the better that your strategy has to evolve. The natural progression of life is that it starts easy and progressively becomes harder. It is much like lifting weights in a gym. The first reps are easy, and then it becomes increasingly more difficult to perform as well as the first reps. Common nature. Keep working and make sacrifices if you have to. Give your time to greater priorities.

The next rule is:

6. Timing.

Things are going to happen and you may not have any control over financial losses and investments. That is just the nature of the game of money. If there were only certainty in making money, what would be the point? We would all be incredibly rich. Money needs an element of time to induce challenge, uncertainty, and risk, or it would not be as powerful as it is. After all, money is a spiritual force. Spirits are free to do what they want. Like any creation, wealth creation takes time. Money is made over time and lost over time. Time will tell how well an investment did and how much time was needed before something was created. The natural progression is that things start simple and over time become progressively harder. Time heals everything and it can also destroy everything. Humans have physical, mental, and emotional pain. Time can also be pain.

Before I continue onto the other rules about money, I would like to inspire new ideas and elements about money.

In business and success, the more successful that you become, the more people that you will naturally attract. As your wealth grows, you have to be more careful with your money. As the tree becomes bigger, the winds become heavier. Money can attract some of the best people into your life and can also attract some of the worst people into your life. We live in a very materialistic society where everyone is after your money. They will try and get it from any way that they can. It will never be anything personal, just business and human nature. Money can change how your friends, your family, and society will look at you.

Money magnifies character to a great degree. What you do with your money is going to show the world what kind of person that you are. How you spend your money will show your morals, your beliefs, and your spirit. When your bank account becomes larger, it will magnify your character even more. Everybody wants money, but not everybody gets money. When you understand the spirit of money, you will be able to attract it into your life. You will be able to be connected to money and its spirit.

The majority of people feel insecure when there is financial instability in their life. Financial security has a way of stabilizing people and their emotions. It breaks my heart, but I have seen many people that were really close to me take a dive off the emotional and mental deep end because of the lack of financial security. Money has a way of taking a toll on people's egos if they are not doing well financially. Money can also inflate someone's ego to a dangerous level. As your wealth grows, your humbleness should grow too. People that have an average to low talent let everyone know that they are great and people with incredible talent tell the world that they are okay. If your confidence is too high, people's expectations of you will be high, which can be dangerous if you fail. If you remain modest and humble, you will blow people away and exceed their expectations because you will not have to match your ego level. People appreciate people that are classy and humble. Always have class and be classy to everyone that you talk to and wherever you go.

In business, sell your story rather than sell your product. The greatest stories create the most sales. Stories make people vulnerable and emotional. When we listen to a story, it opens people up and they buy based on emotion. If your story has compelling content and the listener follows the story, they are more likely to respond emotionally to something. Content is king. If there was a single blank book on the table, people may not purchase it. If the same book had the story that an ancient monarch owned it, it would be much more desirable because of its story. People like when things have a certain feel and meaning to it. Stories are unique and the uniqueness of a story makes the product unique.

Be nice to everyone, because you never know how much money or power someone may have. Some people may be of great value to you if you treat them well. You never know how someone can help you. Do not be nice because you may get something out of it. Be nice anyway. In a social setting, see what you can give rather than what you can receive. Give your attention and focus on what they have to say. It does not matter if they are the most powerful CEO or the poorest person off the street. Treat everyone the same, as we are all one.

In my personal life, the people that I judged and thought were nobody actually were incredibly rich. The people that I thought were somebody actually had nothing. Never judge a book by its cover and never judge a person without giving them the benefit of the doubt that they can enrich your life. To this day, I never judge and it is a huge relief to try and love someone before putting them down. Love eliminates fear. Your network of people is highly important. Your network of people defines who you are to a great degree. Like attracts like. People are more likely to do business with you if you resemble them.

Business in its simplest form is the exchange of value. Value is supply and demand. Scarcity creates value. What value are you annually contributing that satisfies consumers wants? Add so much value that even when you are not at your business, you are still delivering a tremendous amount of value.

How valuable are you?
How valuable is your product or service?
How valuable is your price?
How valuable is your marketing?
How valuable is your story?

In business, you will need to learn sales. You will never close everyone, but you can close most people. Objections are just excuses that you need to overcome. The more excuses and tests that you overcome, the better that you will be in sales. Be a master of your business and be sure to know more about your business than your customer. Find the structure in the non-structure. People need to trust you, your product or service, and your price in order to do business with you. If one of those elements is missing, they will not do business with you.

At the end of the day, it generally boils down to money. People use emotional math to calculate how much time and energy they exercised to acquire their money. If they feel that their time spent earning their money is more valuable than the value of you and your product or service and your price, they will not do business with you. The number one reason that people do not buy is because they do not see the value in parting with their money, even if they can comfortably afford your product or service. Your value has to outweigh their value for them to part with their money. Even after they like you and your product or service, it will always boil down to price. Selling your price to a customer is not a great way to sell value. Focus on the emotional piece, which is your story about the product or service. When you are knowledgeable and skilled at what you do, people will generally like you by default. You need to make sense to them and make them feel comfortable.

In business, you have to deal with gossip and criticism. Gossip and criticism is part of business and will always be present, no matter how great that you are. Not everybody is going to like you. If everybody liked you, what would be the point? People are very affected by reviews, comments, and complaints about their business. Bullying in the work place is a very real thing and the best mechanism that you can learn is to protect yourself from bullying. Do not allow yourself to be bullied. The leader of the business and anyone in the business is subjected to bullying. The media can bully your business too. Everybody is subjected to bullying, especially when someone is succeeding financially.

The sad reality is that most people in life are unsuccessful. Everybody wants to be successful, but something stops a lot of people from becoming successful. Do not bully anyone because you have not walked in his or her shoes and you do not know what they are going through. Unsuccessful people do not want to see others succeed. People often hate others that are doing better than they are. Do not let someone with broken dreams try to dim the shine of your dreams or the successes that you achieve. It does not matter if it is your family, friends, or anybody else. Do not let anybody tell you, "You are not going to make it and that I am only saying this because I love and care for you." The best feeling in the world is to prove people wrong. Success is the best revenge that you could ever deploy. Get rid of the people that do not want to see you succeed. People hate because of something that you have that they do not. Winners want to see others succeed. Haters are needy and want your attention because they lack attention. Ignore the haters.

Influence in business happens because you know somebody, you are somebody, or you have money. No matter what your financial goal may be, make sure that it matches the quality and lifestyle that you want to live. Having a successful life is incredibly difficult, but it is possible. A successful life is a result of you.

You live one life, but you live multiple lives in one.

Your personal life
Your professional life
Your romantic life
Your family life
Your self-development life
Your creative life

You have multiple lives and an endless amount of lives that you could possibly live in this one life that you are living. To become successful, live up to a high quality in your multiple lives. Your life is highly multidimensional. In your one life, you live many lives.

Live a high quality life in your personal life
Live a high quality life in your health life
Live a high quality life in your professional life
Live a high quality life in your financial life
Live a high quality life in your spiritual life

In business, study the evolutions of business and manage the risks. Learn from a business's infancy stage to the more elder stages and the whole cycle of a business. Focus on patterns, because patterns are part of nature. Patterns of past behavior and progression may help you. If you want to invest money, learn how businesses evolve. There is a science of how businesses evolve. Reverse-engineer how any business became successful and you will see the formula and the recipe for success. If your business is on social media, find the viral recipe and replicate it. Creating consistently is huge. In business, the long term is always more important than the short term.

Exposure is important. Keep going until you find what works and what does not work.

To be financially successful, you need to be sensible and intelligent. The most intelligent and the most enlightened people have money, but do not optimize around the exception. If you have financial success, it means that you have understood what people want. People may need something, but they do not want it. People need to eat healthy, but they want to eat unhealthy. People need a roof over their head, but some people do not want that because they would rather live on the street. Needs are essentially wants. Our priority of wants determines the importance of our wants and we call it needs. Everything is a want. Understand what people want, give it to them, and money will flow to you.

Sometimes it does not matter what someone did before, it may matter more what he or she is doing now. Someone may have had a track record of wealth creation 30 years ago, but not now. As time changes, adaptation is required. Business is constantly evolving and some people's business practices are outdated. Live business in the time that you are living. Have a healthy vision of what the future of business will look like.

Be honest and do not be phony. People can see right past dishonesty. In business, do whatever is necessary to succeed. Do not sacrifice your integrity to get something from someone. You will always lose in the end. Business is a 24 hour, 365 days a year war. To do well at war, you must be and do your very best. Work on yourself and you will do better at the game of war of business. Someone else's happiness can contribute to your happiness. Never let someone else's happiness be the sole reason of your happiness. If you make your client, customers, or fans really happy, you may get a sense of happiness that you were able to contribute such a positive and great amount of goodness into their life. Although the game of money is a pay to play game, see everybody as a person. Be nice to customer service people and people that are trying to make a difference, no matter what level that they are on. They are only players of the same game. They are a different version of you and you are a different version of them.

In business, it is important to learn and to understand psychology. Body language can differentiate if someone is successful or unsuccessful. Learn management of people and yourself. There are few leaders in the world and mostly followers. Great leaders inspire followers to become better. As a leader of a business, you can inspire your employees and other workers to feel a sense of purpose and potential for growth. People work harder if they feel that they are valued and not just a number. In negotiation, you need to learn psychology to help you with the verbal and non-verbal cues in people. Understand what people do and why they do what they do. The question "Why" is a powerful word to ask yourself. Understanding "Why" will always be to your benefit.

Money is multidimensional and lives in the past, present, and future. Money is an idea and numbers are invisible. No one can determine the sum of money that you have unless you show him or her your bank account. People that flaunt may not have money and the people that keep low profile may have lots of money. You can make money online, offline, or use the Balance, which is online and offline simultaneously. There are countless ways to make money. You can make money independently or with a team. You can work for money or money can work for you. It is about predicting where the money is going to go. Business is a game that focuses on the long term and is played in the short term. Enough short term creates a long term. Most people know and most people need to be reminded of things that they already know.

When you understand your failures, you will understand your successes. Share your genius with the world and you will be rewarded greatly. I firmly believe that we are all geniuses, and that we all have the capability of bringing out our genius ideas. Genius is a result of slight madness and we all have a bit of madness to us. That is what makes everyone unique. Your madness is different than everyone else's madness.

Like the war of business, it is dangerous to make decisions when you are emotional. Some decisions may need to be made emotionally. Other decisions need to be made non-impulsively and thoughtfully. Your mind, body, and emotions work in harmony. When they are all in harmony, you will attract a better life. Relax the three and you will make better decisions.

Businesses evolve like humans and go through the process of baby, teenager, adult, elder. The health and time of a business can die at anytime. You can save a business and you can save a human through the course of its life. If you neglect the business's needs, it will die. Money is the health and blood of business. Paying customers are what nourish your business. Learn the nature of business. As humans reproduce and have offsprings, businesses scale and grow. Humans and businesses are very similar. You are a business. Your life is a business. It is your business and no one else's business. If you study humans, you can understand a business.

Human health and business health are quite similar. Both are simple and both are quite complex. Humans speak a language and business speaks its own language. In business, it all comes down to one thing and that thing is all about the money.

Business, like language, has many currencies around the world. Business is a universal language. Not everyone is proficient at language or understands language. Business is an art and humans are art. Every human that you see is a piece of artwork, because we are all unique. Every piece of art can be appreciated in some way, shape, or form.

When investing, believe in the business and in the person running the business. Someone can be a lawyer, but if they were not winning cases, why would you invest in that lawyer? In business, you may collaborate with someone or a business with a big audience and an abundance of consumers to help your business. If you are on social media and have few followers and then you're seen on someone else's profile who has millions of followers, you will get the exposure to gain followers on your profile.

People think too big too fast and do not go through with achieving their desired level of income. Our brain is not designed to always be happy. If we were designed to be happy all of the time, what would be the point? Our brain is in constant survival mode and it exaggerates things that could hurt us, such as people's opinions about us. A person or people's opinion of us will not kill you. If something will not kill you, then do not take it so seriously, if at all.

The next rule is:

7. Offence or Defense.

In business, you are either in offensive mode or defensive mode. When you have little money, you logically would tend to be more in offence mode. When you have an abundance of money, you tend to be more on offence and defense mode. As you get richer, you may choose to become more in defense mode. Rich people will never be completely in defense mode. The biggest problem is that people that have little money are in defense mode and not offence mode. They have a scarcity mindset and are trying to defend the little money that they have to survive. They remain in survival mode and defend out of fear. When you have little money, you should silence the fear and not let it paralyze you. Become in offence mode and figure out a way to put yourself in front of people with money.

Consumers tend to have money. Investors tend to have money. Figure a way to give value through your talents or gifts to someone in exchange for money. Start to become in offence mode and figure out a way to attract money into your life without being desperate. Desperation scares money away. Have an idea that will make you money. Get on the Internet, make some phone calls, do what you need to do to make it happen. Think outside the box and you will be able to do it. You can attract anything into your life if you ask for it, believe in it, and work towards getting it.

When you are strictly in defense mode, fear is preventing you from taking action and attracting more money into your life.

When you are in offence mode, you are taking action. When you take action, results happen. Money follows attention and action is attention. Make the transition from complete defense to complete offence. Seek and you shall find. There is a way to make more money, grow your business further, and develop greater. Money is always going up, going down, going up, going down, and going up. There are times where you will have to be in offence mode, and there are times where you will have to be in defense mode.

Become a master of Balance between offence mode and defense mode. Never just be one or the other. Things are forever changing and nothing stays in the same place. Adapt and adjust accordingly. If you want money, become in offence mode, if you want to save money, become in defense mode. You could potentially save more money if you made more money. Saving more by making more is an act of offence and defense at the same time.

Regardless of your financial goals or how well you are doing for yourself, it is going to take you time. You can double, triple, or quadruple your money if you are smart about it. Think about your financial future and all that takes is a little bit of planning and work on your part. Think about the numbers that you want. If you can think the number, you can achieve the number. Become best friends with money and business. Learn more about money and business and you will make more.

If you do not have money, it is because you lack an understanding of the game of money. If you can misunderstand something, you can flip it around and start understanding. You will only become financially better if you make yourself better. It really does not matter what shape the economy, the government, or your environment is, the only difference that matters is yourself. Be in an environment that allows you to dream. If you put in the work, you will make the money. If you put the energy in, the spiritual energy of money will be present in your life. As you grow, your bank account grows.

Focus on what you love and on your purpose and you can turn your whole financial standings right around. As you give more, you will receive more. Give yourself the time to learn about money and business and you will receive money. The more time given to learning and practicing money and business, the more money received as a result of your giving. You can monetize anything.

Change your beliefs to positive ones. Focus and stay motivated. Learn, change, adapt and money will come pouring in, especially if you love the process of what you are doing and not fixating only on the end result. Focus on the now before you see later. The great vision of later is built as a result of the building now. Give without expectation. If you focus your attention on the possibility of achieving great prosperity in the future and you remain non-attached to the outcome, you will achieve it. As it is important to believe that you want ten million dollars in 10 years, you have to act like a person that would make ten million dollars in 10 years. That person would work hard and master their craft and purpose. Anyone can become wealthy. Wealth creation is a result of alteration of thought process and habits.

Now it is time for you to dream of money, and then achieve it. Let money help assist you in acquiring the resources necessary to become the best and most fulfilled version of yourself.

9

Different

You are nearly getting to the end of this book and if you can read an entire book, you can get to the place of your dreams. Few people achieve their dreams just like few people finish reading an entire book. You are already different in the fact that you made it this far into this book. One page at a time got you here. Like completing any goal, it takes one moment at a time.

This chapter is the one that is either going to make you or break you. All of the previous chapters and knowledge will not help you unless you implement this into your life. This is the single most important lesson that will get you to your desired place. You must do things differently than you have done them before. Different actions produce different results. If you do the same things that you have done before, you will produce the same results. If you like the results that you are getting, then keep going. If you are not satisfied with where you are and you want to live a new life with a new meaning, then you have to do things differently.

Be different than anyone else. You were born different than everybody else so you should live differently than everybody else. To be you is the thing that will bring you happiness. People that are not real maintain a false image and become very unhappy only living up to the expectations of other people. Real people do not care about what anybody thinks of their image. Real people know that they are born different than everybody else and they do what feels right to them. When you stop caring about what other people think of you, you start to become happier and your decisions will become a lot more natural. Caring about what other people think is unrealistic and will put unnecessary stress on you.

The truth is, nobody really cares about your life. People care about their own life because people are highly self-important. If someone thinks that you are not cool, would you really want to hang out with them? When someone cannot see the beauty in you, then it is their loss, not yours. Nobody dictates your value or your self-worth. Everybody cares about what other people think. To not care about what other people think is to be different. Life is too short to live up to anybody else's image of how you should be. Take off your mask and be you. Be honest with yourself because you will always win if you are honest with yourself. When you do not care about what other people think, you allow yourself to be you. True happiness and fulfillment comes from being you.

Everybody is different and no two people are the same. Be different because you are different. Think different and embrace different. Embrace difference in yourself and difference in others. Look at every different angle because there is always more than one way of looking at something. There are countless interpretations because everything is so multidimensional. Be different in this loveless, unhealthy, unhappy, poor society that we live in. You can rise to a better quality of life that is different than the way the masses live.

If you want to really change your life and be different, start religiously eating healthy. Poor health is the biggest killer of your dreams. The subtlety of healthy dietary habits will make all the difference for your functionality and focus. We live in a society where people are uneducated about health and basically eat garbage. The unhealthy foods that they eat can cause a serious addiction and craving. Sugar will mess your life up completely. Of course the body needs natural sugar, but get rid of the excess refined white sugar. Make sure that your body remains alkaline and maintains high alkalinity. When your body becomes acidic, sickness will arise. Get in the habit of understanding chemicals and what is put into your food. Know the make-up of your body and what it requires. If you put the wrong fluids in a car, it may not function or may have great problems in the future. Your body is like a car. Like a car, if a tire is under-inflated or over-inflated, it is prone to blow out. Tires must be maintained just right. Not too over-inflated and not too under-inflated. That is Balance.

You do not need a medical degree to live a healthier life. It takes a little work to understand the fundamentals of health. Like anything, the basic knowledge of a subject will take you a long way. When you are eating a healthy diet, you can prevent many things. Many diseases are completely preventable based on eating properly and giving your body the requirements that it needs. When you start to learn about a healthy diet and health as a whole, you will completely change your life. The way that you think, feel, and handle your emotions will be much more easily managed. Eating healthy should not be a trend to show off, but a lifestyle habit that is essential to your wellbeing and success. Getting to your dream and not having a high level of health is not ideal. You want to be healthy when you reach your goal. Your goal could be to have a big beautiful house one day and what is the point if you cannot enjoy your home because you do not have good health? Your first wealth is your time. Your second wealth is your health. Never sacrifice your health for wealth.

The break through moment in my personal life was eating healthy. Ever since I stopped eating processed foods and going to most restaurants, my thoughts, emotions, and moods altered. As my health and body became better, my mind and soul followed. The body, mind, and soul work best in harmony with each other. The best part about becoming healthy through diet is that you become emotionally stable and happier.

If you are tired, it is likely because you are dehydrated. Hydrating will super-charge your energy levels. As your energy levels rise, you will become much more productive. As you become more productive, you will head in the direction of your dreams and end goals.

Be different. Most people change for the short term and go back to their old ways that they were previously living. As you know, if you do what you did previously, you will end up with the exact same results. When you change, make sure that it is a lasting change. The idea is to go forward. What is the point of changing in the short term? Create a lasting change by consistently maintaining the change and keeping the change in check. If you become lazy, you will eventually go back to your previous results.

When you do different things, you take on a different life. Do something that you have never done before, especially if it scares you. Think about: What if you did things differently? Why are you going to do things differently? What are you going to do differently? How are you going to do things differently? What difference do you want to see in yourself or your world?

When you do things differently, do not dwell on the past, focus on the future. You are not in your past anymore. Do not think about what did not work before. Think about what could work now and onwards. You are building towards the future right now. The current present will always be the future's past. Learn how decisions are going to affect you. Learn how decisions are going to affect others. Learn how decisions will affect the environment. Decision-making is critical to being different, living different, and exposing you to different experiences. Decisions can make you and break you. Every decision is yours and you need to own up to the decisions that you make. Decisions will be made real in the future if you act on your decisions.

Everything is based on your previous patterns. Fortunately, you can change your patterns now to create new patterns. For the most part, people do not change because they hate change by their nature and because it is easy to live naturally and not create lasting change. People avoid discomfort, but it is through discomfort that change and difference occurs. Lasting change takes too much work for people because they are lazy and scared to exercise the proper discipline to keep up with their change. If you keep up with a positive new change, over time it will become a habit.

The natural progression of things is that it starts simple, then gradually progresses harder, then becomes easier, then it becomes harder, then easier and so fourth. Back and forth, back and forth like a fluttering needle between the two binaries to remain in the Balance. If something does not fluctuate up and down, or side-to-side, and remains straight, it is dead. Good and evil are in constant battle to create the Balance. That is why you will be happy, then sad, then happy, then sad. All the other emotions between happy and sad are the Balance between the two binaries of happy and sad. That is why things in the universe are always changing because they are alive. Sometimes even mathematical laws. However, math remains the same because it has the stability of numbers. Numbers change, but numbers are constant.

People do not like change, but we all want to become better. Everything in nature is evolving. Things evolve to get better. It is in our very nature to get better. Do not delay the process to evolve yourself. When you become different in your thoughts, actions, and decisions, you will evolve. The whole goal of life is to evolve.

Your definition of success is going to be unique to you. It is going to be different than anyone else. What success means to you may not mean success to someone else. What success means to someone else may not mean success to you. We are all so different. You can define success anyway that you want. Apply the definition of success to your life by living different to achieve different.

Nobody does things better than you. They just do it differently than you. We are all the same, we are all one, but different. You are a different version of everyone and everyone is a different version of you. Different things have different meanings. No two lives will have lived the same, only different. You can live differently. If you are on the flip side, you can live on the flop side. It does not matter what anyone thinks. Your success is about you and your growth.

Most people feel entitled to everything. Be different and realize that you are not entitled to anything unless you work for it. The sooner you realize that life owes you nothing, you will start taking greater accountability. There are no shortcuts to a successful life and growth. Nobody grows from a baby to 6 feet tall in one night. There is nothing new that is created by doing the same thing. When there are no challenges, there is no growth or opportunity to evolve.

If you want to do well in business, you need to understand that money is a documented receipt of your time and your talents. If you want a great receipt, you are going to have to do things differently to develop yourself, your company, your brand, your thoughts, your methods, your principles, your beliefs, and your culture.

When you do things differently, it is important to maintain a relaxed, and calm state of mind. Do not panic and make things worse than they are. Things are never as bad as you think that they are. Success is freedom to live your life the way that you want. Live differently now and you will live differently later. Live the same now and you will live the same later.

Money gives you different options and different choices. You can throw money at most of your problems. If you have a car that needs maintenance, the best way to fix that problem is to throw money at it. Then you no longer have that problem. When you throw money at a problem and the problem subsides, things will be better and easier for you. It will free up your time. There is no such thing as cheating because you threw money at a problem. Not all problems can be fixed with money, but if it can be fixed, why not fix it? Make it easier on yourself.

In life, there are no coincidences or accidents. There is no such thing as luck. Everything happens for a reason no matter how good or how bad that it may be. You may not exactly know the reason why something happened, but it serves a greater purpose beyond yourself if you do not understand it right away. Experience will always be more valuable than theory. You can study something all your life, but until you actually do it and find out for yourself, you will not really know. To really be happy, contribute to yourself and to your talents. If you are depressed, start giving more to others.

If you feel like what you are giving does not feel much of value, give differently. There is more than one way to give to the world. There are many ways. Give honestly. Honest people do not need to justify themselves. When you look at things from a different perspective, the once impossible becomes possible. If you can envision it, it will always be possible. It only takes that one perspective to change everything. Look at the perspective that says that it is possible. Throw the word impossible out of your dictionary.

There is sanity in the insanity and there is insanity in the sanity. If you are lost, start from the basics and work from the ground up. Start simple, and sometimes you will have to rethink in a simple way to reinvent something differently. If you want a different life, go back to the basics. What do you love? Do not think about what you like, but about what you love. Make the things that you love present in your professional life. We spend quite a bit of time in our professional lives. If you do things that do not positively stimulate your mind and your emotions, over time you will be unhappy. Make sure that your professional life aligns with the things that you love and that bring you a great amount of joy and passion. If you do more of the things that you love in your professional life, you will feel more fulfilled and happy.

If you do not like working with numbers professionally, why would you pick a profession that is strictly about numbers? No amount of money is worth your suffering. Most people take a job without thinking much about it and they become unhappy over time. The quality of profession that contributes to your happiness is the one that you should do and the money will follow.

There is always more than one way to accomplish something. Success is achieved in more than just one way. Society wants you to conform to it. Be different, think different, and act different than society. People become unhappy when they try to maintain an image. Live your life and take risks. You need very little to survive on this planet. Food, water, shelter is all you need. If you want to try something different, shadow someone that is doing what it is that you want to do. You may love it or not love it. If you do not love it, do not do it. Your happiness is your primary purpose. Your business needs to reflect you and you need to reflect your business.

My purpose is to give. One of the biggest reasons why I like to help people is to watch as their eyes light up because they now know what is possible that they did not see in themselves before. This is different because most people do not help anybody but themselves. As it is important to help yourself, you must give service to people to truly feel fulfilled. Business is evidence that you must give. You must go and see what you can give rather than what you can receive. Give more than you receive. Most people are takers. If most people realized the joy and fulfillment of giving, the world would be a lot happier and a more fulfilled place.

Now it is time for a moment of truth. Time to be different.

Not happy with your relationship or marriage? Change it.
Not happy with your life? Change it.
Not happy with your friends? Change it.
Not happy with your job? Change it.
Not happy with how your business is running? Change it.
Not happy with your thoughts? Change it.
Not happy with your wardrobe? Change it.
Not happy with your car? Change it.
Not happy with your music? Change it.
Not happy with your health? Change it.
Not happy with your income? Change it.
Not happy with your sadness? Change it.
Not happy with your environment? Change it.
Not happy with your present? Change it.
Not happy with being shy? Change it.
Not happy with your room? Change it.
Not happy with your parenting? Change it.
Not happy with your diet? Change it.
Not happy with your major? Change it.
Not happy with your decision? Change it.
Not happy with the way people treat you? Change it.
Not happy with negativity? Change it.
Not happy with drama? Change it.

Not happy with your credit? Change it.
Not happy with your body? Change it.
Not happy with your social media account? Change it.
Not happy with your daily routine? Change it.
Not happy with the same results? Change it.
Not happy with your social life? Change it.
Not happy with your love life? Change it.
Not happy with something? Change it.
Not happy with you? Change you.

You are in control of your life to a greater extent than you can imagine. You can choose the quality of your life. You can choose if you are going to live out your dream or not. You can choose what kind of people are around you. You can choose what places you go to. You can choose the things in your life. You choose, not anyone else. If you think someone else is in control of your destiny, you are heavily mistaken. You have unlimited power to get out of the rut that you are in. It only takes a little creativity to change your situation and circumstances. To change is to do things differently and to do things differently is to change. Change comes from doing things differently. From the color of your shirt, to your sex life, to where you live, to whom that you see, to what you do. Everything is subject to change. You control the change and differences in your life, nobody else.

The more control over your life that you believe that you have, the more control that you will feel that you have. When you feel that you have control, it is because you have control. You control you. Life is still going to happen because by nature it is continuously trying to evolve everything. Mother nature wants to nurture and grow everything and everyone. You cannot control everything that happens to you, but you can control what happens because of you. Life is magnetic. What you want to happen will happen, but it may happen in a different way. If nobody could achieve what they wanted, what would be the point? Nobody would be trying if nobody were ever successful.

Go somewhere that you have never been before
Try a new restaurant that you have not dined at before
Meet someone that you have never met
Try a new hobby or activity that you have never tried
Try a different way than what you normally do
Go a different route
Order a new item
Try to find new websites
Find other people that do what you love
Join a different organization
Go to a different music venue
Do something at a different time
Look at your business from a different viewpoint
Imagine how things are without any sound
Put yourself in your customer's shoes
Sign up for a new gym
Shop somewhere different
Try to develop a different habit
Try to develop a different thought
Think differently about something
Believe that maybe something is not too good to be true
Download new apps on your phone
Listen to different music

Minor creativity creates a majorly different life. Fear is the only thing that would stop you because humans are afraid of being uncomfortable and of change. Embrace the new and potential whole new world. If you are not open to change and evolving, then you will never achieve your greatest dream. If you are willing to change and be different, you will be able to get to your greatest dream eventually.

See how others live their life differently than you. Expose yourself to the different and you will become different. Different always makes you evolve better. Fear is the only thing that gets in the way of a difference. Emotionally manage the fear while doing a new action. Find the different. The difference makes the difference. Keep exposing yourself to the different and you will become different. When you become different, your life becomes different. You can start the next new chapter of your life.

Be a mad scientist of your life and experiment with new things. People become depressed because they are not experimenting. Curiosity will drive you to be different. Take on a sense of curiosity in your life to find the different. A different life caused by different events and encounters will bring you different outcomes. When you create different outcomes for yourself, anything is possible. One different outcome is achieving your dream. You are one different outcome away of achieving your dream. One outcome could multiply into many outcomes like the ripples of a drop in the water. Outcomes can be short or long, big or small.

Do not be afraid of failure because the worst outcome is that somebody says "No". For every "No" that you get, you are one step closer to an inevitable "Yes". When you do things that are different, you will fail. Humans are scared of failure and they associate failure with loss. Failure should be associated with gain. When the failures are doubled, the successes are doubled. When the failures are tripled, the successes are tripled. It is a mathematical law of the universe.

When you fail, you become better and stronger. You learn more and become more knowledgeable. When you do things differently, it will cause you to fail. Get a good feel of failing and fail often. You cannot do anything great if you do not expose yourself to failure. Failure is a friend and is not the enemy. When you try new experiences, you will fail. Through your failures is where you will grow and develop yourself. What is the worst that can happen? You learn something new. Try, try, and try again. Create different outcomes for yourself by doing things differently. Different outcomes can better or worsen your life. It does not matter what your presumption of the outcomes are, it just matters to experiment and see what works and what does not. Exhaust all possibilities. If all you have tried was one food, how do you know what any other food will taste like?

Do not enable yourself to think that you do not know something. You do know, and it starts by doing. Engage in the unknown and live in the unknown. You know what is best for you deep down. You are smarter than you will ever give yourself credit for. Look deep down within and you will pull it out of you. Close your eyes and imagine what is possible by doing things differently.

Change your behavior, mindset, and way of life. When you look at things differently, the things that look different change. Get as many new experiences as you possibly can. Through experience, you will grow. New experiences lead to meeting new people, development of new skills, and acquiring new wisdom. All it takes is creativity to get out of your bubble and start a new journey to help you progress towards your dream.

The mathematical law will always be:
The same thing will always get you the same thing
The different thing will always get you the different thing

The choice is yours. It is completely binary if you want to change or not. Your differences are going to make you unique. Imagine doing something that you have never done before. Imagine how emotionally compelling it could be. Perhaps it may not be as great as you think the experience will be, but there is only one way to find out. Be bold and do things differently. If you think that you cannot do things differently, take a freezing cold shower. Run somewhere, then beat the distance the next day. See what other people are doing. See the structure in the non-structure. One difference can completely change your life and allow you to live up to a higher quality. Enhance the quality of your life through changes.

Spend some alone time and go to the drawing board. Think about what could be. Research and write down some things that you would like to try and then act on your curiosity. Curiosity will drive you right to your dreams. When you become curious about your dream, your dream becomes curious about you. When you become curious about life, life becomes curious about you. When you take action and act on the things that you are curious about, you will try new things. New things create a new life. Do not be scared of change. Change can always be for better or for worse. Positively focus on what could be better rather than what could be worse. Positive attracts positive and negative attracts negative. Positive needs negative and negative needs positive. There is good in the bad and there is bad in the good. Positive thoughts and ideas are the main focus.

Fear, laziness, and lack of ideas are the only things keeping you back from living a different life. If you become fearless, proactive, and create a solid idea, you can create a new life. Life was designed to create. Everything in life is a creation. You create your mind and your world. Create as much as you can. Master creation and then you will be able to create your dreams into existence. Every creation started with a single thought before it was built into existence. Dig deep down and think of what you want different. What could you do differently? Is there something that you have been curious about? Curiosity breeds curiosity. When you become more curious about things, then there will be more things to be curious about. Once your curiosity teaches you something, that knowledge will give you the power to tackle bigger things that you will be curious about. Curiosity multiplies. You will never know everything in this lifetime.

Life will always give you things to be curious about if you actively seek to find more. As your curiosity grows, life will give you greater mysteries to solve. The way that we learn is through curiosity. It is the single best thing to implement in your thought process. If you are not curious about the possibilities of things and outcomes, you will not learn anything. When you do not learn, you do not grow. When you do not grow, you do not evolve into the next stage. Everything has a domino effect. The mind was created to be curious. A curious mind that is active evolves. As you become more curious about different results and different ideas, you will continue to evolve. When you evolve, you always evolve for the better, not worse. If you evolved for the worse, you would devolve. As long as you allow your curiosity to drive you to do different things, you will evolve. If you do nothing, you will remain the same or you will devolve.

When your life becomes different, you will experience different. Different creates different. People that are unhappy and unfulfilled generally are doing the same things. When you do the same things and produce the same results, you will feel like you are not going anywhere and you will not feel happy. When there is change, it gives you something to look forward to. Relight the spark in your life by creating a difference. People always want to feel as if they are progressing towards something to feel happy. If they do not, they become quite unhappy.

When you try new things, your whole life takes on a different meaning and then you will feel like you are progressing towards something. When you walk in the direction of new, things become newer. When you walk in the direction of old, things become older. Walk in the direction of new. Old is the past and new is the future. Do not live in the past because it will not help you to live in the future. You cannot change the past, but you can change the present to realize a new future. You can have a different life and live differently a lot sooner than you think. Today you could do something differently that will make tomorrow very different.

Different is present and future based. The past can be different than what is now, but it remains the same. The more different that you live today, the more different your tomorrow will be. If you do the same thing for the rest of your life that is not serving you, you will become very unhappy. The beauty about change is that you can make big changes or you can make small changes. Do things a little differently or a lot differently. People are very Black and White and think that they need to do something radical to change. That is not true. If you set your alarm for 7:00am today, and 6:30am tomorrow, you have already made a different change. You got up a half an hour earlier. That is a small difference. You do not need to get up at 4:00am. That is too extreme of a difference too quickly.

Gradually and incrementally is the best way to create lasting change and to create a different life. People are way too extreme too fast. The natural progression of life is to start simple then gradually progress harder. If you are not used to going to the gym and then you impulsively went seven days a week 2 hours a day, you would probably end up hurting yourself. If you started 2 to 3 days a week in the beginning, you would make a positive and sensible change. There are times where you are going to have to jump in the deep end quickly, but not every change needs to be that quick. It is best to start a change gradually. Today, you could go to bed a half an hour earlier. That would be making a different change gradually. That would be healthy because you would not disturb your circadian rhythm.

If you lifted 100 pounds and you have never lifted 40 pounds in your life, you will hurt yourself. You must build up before you can lift 100 pounds. The same is true while making changes. When people change too fast, they end up feeling disappointed that they could not create a positive change that was lasting. They were different momentarily, but could not sustain the different. More often than not, it is best to test the waters. Learn to walk before you learn to run. Every new experience is learning to walk. How could you join a professional sport team if you have never played the sport before?

With proper discipline, dedication, and a plan, any change can be a lasting one. You always need to have a plan. You may not know exactly the way the plan will unfold, but you need to make a mathematical approximation close to the desired outcome.

Life is highly mathematical and without the proper planning and preparedness, failure is certain.

Your business approaches can be different
Your relationship approaches can be different
Your job approaches can be different

Your health approaches can be different
Your thought approaches can be different
Your emotion approaches can be different
Your hobby approaches can be different
Your dream approaches can be different
Your experience approaches can be different
Your travel approaches can be different
Your diet approaches can be different
Your time approaches can be different
Your sleeping approaches can be different
Your practice approaches can be different
Your research approaches can be different
Your success approaches can be different
Your happiness approaches can be different
Your interpretation approaches can be different

If you can think it, you can make it different. Anything and every-thing is subject to change and to being different. You have the influence to make them different. Approach from up to down, down to up, right to left, and left to right. There are multiple approaches to everything and life is highly multidimensional. You may not see it now, but it can be seen. You may not see it, but it can see you. Just like your dreams. You cannot see your dreams, but they can see you. Eventually, you will be able to see your dream eye to eye in reality time. You are only here until you become there. You are only there until you become here.

In my life, I could purposefully hallucinate my dream pictured in my head. Only through an incredible amount of hard work, persistence, being different, discipline, planning, dedication, and overcoming failures, I could one day live out one of my dreams. It is the most euphoric feeling of energy in the world when you dreamt about something every day and then one day that dream became a reality. I could only define completing a dream as the feeling of being in love. The only way that you will get there is to be different then you were before. To be on the correct path, do what most people would not do. If you know that most people would have given up by now, then that means that you have to keep going. If you know that most people would be scared, then that means that you must take action and do it anyway. If you know that most people would only dream of it, then you need to live it.

Get out of your head and lose your mind. You can change your whole life and destiny if you would just invest the time in yourself to make meaningful changes. You have read this far into this book. Most people would have given up way before the half way mark of any book that they would have picked up. You are doing something differently already. Apply that same difference into other aspects of your life. If you want a better income, you have to do things differently. When you do something differently in your profession, you will create a different income. If you do the same work, you will create the same income. Make a change and take the change.

Do what nobody else is doing. Do what you are not even doing. Do not compare yourself to anyone else because your changes are your changes. Do not care about what anyone will think of your different life. You have no competition. The only competition that you have is yourself. Focus on evolving yourself, for your life, for you.

Imagine walking on the sidewalk dressed in a suit or dress. Nobody really pays attention. Now imagine walking on the same sidewalk dressed in the same suit or dress except this time, you are walking with a full-grown pig attached to a leash nonchalantly. All of a sudden, everybody notices. Although it would be cool to walk with a pig by your side, that is not the point. The point is, a subtle difference can make all the difference. See how a new outcome was created? One change in your life could change everything. If you had not walked with the pig, nobody would have paid that close attention to you. One thing makes all the difference. What different things are you doing in your life to produce different results?

Anyone can make a difference in his or her life if they just think differently, act differently, feel differently, or experience differently. Nobody is telling you to change into something that you are not, but change can create a more enhanced version of you. Make yourself evolved into a better version of you. If you have to change into something that you are not, then it may not be the best to change. Sometimes, you do not know if you are something or not. You may think that something is not you, but it is totally you. You may think that something is you, but it is totally not you. The best approach is to know yourself as best as you can and follow your instincts. Always follow your gut because your gut tells you things that the mind cannot. Approach things that you like and from a place of love in anything that you do.

The happiest people in the world are the ones that are open to difference and change. The people that cannot embrace change, fear, or trying different things are usually unhappy. There are always exceptions, but for the most part, this is true. If you try something different and you strongly dislike the outcome, at least you know. You know yourself a little better now than before. If you strongly like the new outcome of something that you did differently, at least you know. You know yourself a little better now than before. It is a win-win situation either way, so what have you got to lose?

Failure is not trying anything new or giving up completely. If you fail and keep going, then it was only a stepping-stone to get to something even better. If you remain the same and are not evolving, then you are failing. To fail is the process of evolving. If you are not failing, you are not evolving. Life has lots in store for you and it is up to you to go to that store and see what is within. Although it is great to be happy with your accomplishments and achievements, it is encouraged to push your limits and excel in your life. Go for greatness and do not settle for just good. Good enough is good in life sometimes, but in your life, greatness should be your goal. You were born in the greatest way and you should live the greatest way. Most people settle for good and do not reach great. Be different than most people and do not settle for good. Go for great. Get the best and forget the rest. Be the very best that you can be. Give it your all because one day you will be dust. When you are dust, it is better to have given it your all than to have regrets.

You will never achieve greatness by remaining the same. When you are greatly different, you will achieve greatness. Greatness with humbleness is the optimal life to live. When you are living up to your greatest self, you do not have to prove anything to anyone. You should not have to prove anything to anyone anyway, except for yourself. Greatness speaks for itself and success is louder than words. If you want to be great, lose your mind and persistently become different. Good is the same and great is the difference.

To live your dream is different than what most people experience and I say go for it. Your whole physiology and spirit will soar to the greatest heights known. Life is only one test, and you only have one shot to do great on that test. You are living the greatest movie ever called, "Life". Focus and you will get there. Hyper focus your mind and forget about everything. Look deep within your soul and execute to achieve greatness. Once you are great, maintain greatness.

You were born different, to live different, to be different, to think different, and to achieve different. It all starts and ends with you. Create different in your life now.

10

Love

Love is acceptance, freedom, and unconditional. Love is the most powerful force in the universe. Love is a rare thing in this world and it is important to give love and to get love. If you do not give and receive love, you will be miserable. Love is a basic human need. It all comes down to loving yourself. You cannot become successful without loving yourself. Until you love yourself, you will not achieve your greatest dreams. If you cannot love yourself, how are you going to love others? Love yourself, then love others, and then love the world.

The truth is that most people hate themselves. When they hate themselves, that toxicity poisons everyone around them. Few people truly love themselves in a healthy way. People intentionally and unintentionally hate themselves. When you are sad and depressed, you are feeding negativity into your mind. When your mind is negative, you will physically become sick as a result. Positive is love. Negative is hate. People love to hate and hate to love.

True happiness and fulfillment comes from being you. There are countless ways to love yourself and to care for yourself in a much deeper and more spiritual level. The first step in loving yourself is to raise your standards and only have high standards for yourself.

One of the best ways to raise your standards is to eat healthy. When you eat healthy, you are giving your body the nutrients that it needs. Eating healthy is the most effective way to love your self. When you eat mostly unhealthy, you are not loving yourself. It is reasonable to seldom eat moderately unhealthy foods, but your diet should comprise of mostly healthy things. Hydrating your body is also a way to increase the love for yourself.

When you learn, grow, and persevere for a solution to one of your problems, you are creating love for yourself. When you are not focusing on the problem and become solution based, you are looking out for yourself. If you focus on the problem and not the solution, you are not helping yourself. To help yourself is to love yourself. To love is to care. If you neglect yourself, that is not loving yourself. Love yourself and make yourself happy. Do what you love. If you did not have to make a living and you could do anything, what would you do? If you are not doing what you love then the question to you is, "Why not?"

You have to love yourself and put yourself into situations that will help you to grow and achieve success. When you love yourself, you will find yourself in positions to win no matter how long or painful the process may be. Your will needs to be strong to complete something. Do something you love even if it means that you will have to suffer for it. Love breeds more love and hate breeds more hate.

Change your environment and make it happen. If you want the opportunity to succeed, you have to go for it. Doing what you want to do is love. Write a love letter to yourself describing in great detail why you are going to do something. Read it, then go and do that. You do not need to stand in front of a mirror and tell yourself that you are beautiful and that you love yourself. Sometimes things just are.

Everyone experiences a great deal of trauma in life. Trauma helps us to evolve. Accept the fact that no matter what happened to you in the course of your life, that you are worthy of loving yourself. Love and move forward. Everyone is worthy of loving themselves. The creator of the universe loves you very much. Anyone that says that there is no creator of the world is ignorant. You are allowed to believe what you want to believe, but something had to create the beautiful nature around you. There was a tremendously powerful force of love poured into existence to create this beautiful universe and the stars above.

There is much evil and wickedness in this world, but it serves a purpose beyond comprehension. The evil needs to Balance the love. Love will always be stronger and louder. When you love yourself, you will be honest with yourself. No matter how harsh the truth is to swallow, you will come clean to yourself. The truth is hard to swallow before you are able to accept it. Never lie to yourself or distort the truth to justify something to yourself. Be completely honest. The truth hurts, but the truth is love.

Verbalize things to yourself and feel your emotions. I do not care how masculine you think you are or how tough you think you are. To express emotion is to be human. You are strong to not repress your emotions and to feel them. Cry if you have to. Weakness is to lie to yourself and keep your emotions from yourself. When you love yourself, you will allow yourself to feel your honest emotions. If you do not feel comfortable crying in front of someone, let the tears run down your face in private. Deal with your emotions because pain does not go away unless you process it head on. Go deep down and rise above the emotions and pain that you are experiencing.

Be you and love yourself. Do not conform to a society that is trying to make you conform. Living how you want is to love yourself. Give up the things that are bad for you. People can be bad for you, food can be bad for you, places can be bad for you, situations can be bad for you, and pleasures can be bad for you. Eliminate the things that no longer serve you. As you start loving yourself and believe in yourself more, life will love you more. Hate is the next emotion to love. As you love yourself, people will start to love you. People can see that you value yourself and they will be more inclined to value you too. Do not accept things that alter your positive view of yourself.

When you love yourself, you will be able to achieve your goals and dreams. Close your eyes and fantasize. Imagine how different your life would be. If someone is a high achiever, they have a high viewpoint of themselves. When you believe in yourself, you will develop the confidence necessary to complete things. You need to be confident to complete something. If you are unconfident about something, you will not finish it. At least you will not finish it well.

When you have certainty in your ability, you will achieve. To have certainty, you must believe in yourself. The best way to love yourself is to love yourself first. Stop trying to please everyone else before pleasing yourself. If you love yourself, you have the potential to love a greater amount of people around you in your life. Love creates love. Do not become narcissistic to the point that no one wants to be around you. You have to love yourself not too much and not too little. Everything requires Balance. Love yourself more than less. The proper amount of love for yourself requires you to have high standards for yourself and to not passively accept things that do not serve your life. If it is not helping you grow your life, it is helping you hinder your life.

The most dangerous weapon in the world along with love is the human mind. Feed the mind. Do not neglect the mind. Your brain was designed to learn and so it should learn frequently. Do not be ignorant, get educated about the world.

A healthy mind is a curious mind. Learn what is going on in the world. Expand and broaden your horizons. Learn to think for yourself and to make decisions for yourself. Make sure that you are independent and are well informed. There are always three people in life. Leaders, followers, and the people that said, "What happened?" Be a leader of your life. Do not be dependent on others. Take charge of your life. Learn to learn. Learn to do critical thinking for yourself and do not take other people's word for something. Just because something is said, does not mean that it is true.

Media, Government, Police, Friends, Family, Doctors, Lawyers, Psychologists, Employers, Celebrities...it does not matter who it may be. People are people and are not perfect. Some people absolutely do not have your best interest in mind or in heart. Never agree with one side of the story if you do not know the other side of the story. Once you know both sides of the story, make your own decision before committing based on facts. To love your self is to inform yourself. Do not follow the herd and jump on the bandwagon.

We as a culture have run into serious problems because people are mostly followers and do not think on their feet for themselves. Ask yourself, "Is this believable?" You need to wake up and realize that what appears to be may not be at all. Protect yourself by becoming well educated. To protect your self with knowledge is to love yourself. If you are naïve or lack proper information, it can seriously harm you. What you do not know will hurt you the most. Be a master of gathering information and facts. I believe in documentation over conversation any day. Ask questions.

Life is beautiful no matter what and each day is worth living. Each day is a vacation that you are above ground and you can learn. To love your self is to carry the highest standards and to not accept anything less. Know your worth because your worth is priceless. You are worth a lot to me even if I do not know you personally. You are worth something to me because you picked up this book in an attempt to better your life and to realize your full potential. You know that your dreams and goals are possible and that you are going to make them happen. There is no question of if, but when.

Love yourself and everything will fall into place. Anything that helps you evolve is creating more love for yourself. There is tough love that you will experience through your failures and that is completely necessary for growth and for change. When you love yourself, you can attract someone into your life who loves themselves too. When two people love and understand themselves, then it becomes possible to love another human being on a deeper personal and spiritual level. Romantic love is best when two people who love themselves are a complement to one another. If you do not love yourself first, your future relationships will suffer. A relationship is to give and to build together. Through relationships, you learn and grow. Good relationships can help to evolve you.

Love is not hard and it is easier to love than to hate. It takes a lot more energy to hate something than to love something. Find the beauty in something rather than look for the ugly in something. See the goodness in yourself rather than the badness in yourself. Focus on the good. You can make the badness better if you have minor creativity and the willingness to develop. Loving yourself can happen quickly. Success is not overnight. Success may happen overnight, but do not focus on the exceptions. Real and meaningful success takes time and it is not a destination, but a continued act.

You may be successful today and unsuccessful tomorrow. Work and maintain success. Love and believe in yourself. No matter what you learn, if you even learn one thing, you are better than you were before. Your life is your story. It is not anybody else's story. Your self-love is not a result of someone else's love, but only of your love. When you accept yourself for what you are, how you look, how you communicate, how you learn, you will be on the right path. Feel the pain of your emotions and hopeless situations and it will pass. To feel is to be human. Love yourself and your ingenious brain. Take care of yourself. Think positively about yourself.

If you love yourself, you will not talk badly about yourself. If someone talked about you the way that you talk about you, would you hang out with that person? Forgive yourself and be kind to yourself. If you feel like you do not love yourself, act as if you love yourself. Sooner or later you will start to believe it. We believe what we tell ourselves repeatedly. Be careful what you put into your mind.

When you love yourself, you will not care about what other people say about you, because you already accept yourself. Love is protection. Nobody can hurt you if your love shields the words of others. Do not be needy, insecure, desperate, or fearful. It causes what you want to disappear. Develop an abundance mindset and not a scarcity mindset. When you are abundant, you will not worry or doubt yourself because whatever you want will always be there. When you are scarce, your fear will attack your positivity and beliefs. When you love yourself, you will not feel the need to attach onto something because your love is constant no matter what the outcome may be. Of course, we all have things that we are insecure about. When you love yourself, insecurities can be managed and overcome. Your imperfections make you beautiful. If you were perfect in every aspect, what would be the point?

You were put here to love yourself and to do what you love. You were designed to give love and to get love. Love is the purpose of why things are possible. It is the force that holds everything together. If all else fails, give love. When you give love, you give great gratitude and appreciation for the world. The world needs more love, as it is a rare thing. Once you have love for yourself, then it is time for the next step. The next step is to love everyone around you.

It does not matter how good or how bad people are. Love them unconditionally, because they are your race of humankind. It does not matter what they look like, how they talk, where they came from, or what they believe in. We all share the same planet and we are all citizens that are coexisting in this universe. Love is beyond racism, hatred, violence, war, destruction, chaos, and terror. Love has no bias. In romantic relationships, to love is to desire. Beyond romantic relationships, love has no bias. Love is love. Love is genderless and is accepting. When human beings learn that the power of love is freedom, the world will know and experience peace and things will never be the same.

Love each day, love each moment, love each person, and love everything equally. Forgive everything. To forgive is to love. We are only here for a short time and there is no time for hatred and despair. A powerful force of love, by love, and for love, created the people of the world. Before we focus on the world, we must focus on ourselves to love and care for one another. We cannot die and leave hatred in the world. Even if you can treat one person that you normally do not like better than you normally do, you are making a difference. You do not need to be best friends, but you must show respect, compassion, and care.

Once we love each other as one, then we can take care of the world. Love the world and the world will love us. We are completely destroying the world and we need to stop. We need to love the world. If you can pick up even 5 pieces of litter off the ground a week, you will be giving love to the world. When we start taking responsibility together, the world will be a better place. It is not one person's job to help the world. It is everybody's job to contribute. We are all here together.

Live your life how you want to live it. If you are not hurting anybody, then do what you want to do. Do what you want, how you want. It is nobody else's business how you live your life. Your happiness comes first. To love your self is to make yourself happy. There is no right or wrong way to live your life because your life is your life.

I can only suggest things in this book. You are going to live your life and do what you are going to do. Try your best to see it through yourself that if you love yourself, anything is possible. Love is always going to be your greatest strength and the thing that will help you fight for your life. You will achieve the life of your dreams through love. When you do something from a place of love, you will never lose.

In business, do not think about how you can make money from a person. Instead, think "How can I love this person better?" Through caring and giving them what they want, you will receive what you want. Love is the greatest value commodity in the universe. Why would you not use love in business? When you ask questions from a loving point of view, it opens windows and possibilities. Love is value and value is business. When you ask how you can love someone better, you are thinking of a way to add greater value to someone's life. When you add great love and value to someone else's life, you reap the rewards.

Be patient with yourself. Understand yourself. Believe in yourself. When you do not love yourself, you will look for someone or something else to believe in. If you do not love yourself and believe in yourself, you are more likely to be manipulated. Have security and confidence in yourself and in your abilities. Although it is healthy to pressure yourself to grow and to evolve, you must be patient with yourself.

Everyone starts as a beginner in anything that they pursue. Some people learn faster, others learn slower. Do not measure yourself based on how fast someone else is succeeding. You are where you are supposed to be. Right now, you are meant to be here and right here. Focus on the now. Nobody is born great until they acquire the confidence from practicing over and over again. Love yourself and always be kind to yourself. Take care of yourself.

Everything will fall into place once you start to love yourself and embrace yourself. If you neglect yourself, yourself will neglect you. You were given one body, mind, and soul. Appreciate the short life that you have been given and love the skin that you are in. You were put here for a great reason so make your reason for being here a great one. Love will always win. You will be spending the rest of your life with yourself, so you should love yourself. You spend the most time with yourself. You spend every moment in your flesh and bones. Your body is the vessel that carries your spiritual soul and your soulful spirit. Stand up for yourself and make things the way that you want them to be.

When you love yourself, you will accept your failures and successes much more powerfully. The love for yourself will carry forward the belief that everything is going to be all right and things are only going to get better from here. Loving yourself gives you a sense of purpose because you can always navigate back onto the right path again.

Once you start to love, accept, and understand yourself, you will begin to understand the world and universe around you. When you have taken care of yourself, you will not have to worry about yourself and you can start learning more about the universe. The universe is offering you everything. It is for you to see it. As you exercise a greater amount of gratitude and appreciation for yourself, the universe will continually give you more to be thankful for having. You attract everything in this universe to your life that you focus on. When you focus on love and loving yourself, more things will come into your life to sustain that love. Love attracts love. When you focus on something and you have the emotionally compelling inspiration to take continued action, you will achieve anything. Do not wait for something to happen, just do it because you love it and you want it in your life. Keep exhausting your failures until the universe has no choice but to surrender the success to you.

You have to be stubborn. When you really love yourself, you will be stubborn. When you remain stubborn in your vision to achieve your dream, you will not change your attitude. That attitude will focus on succeeding the vision. When you are stubborn, it means never giving up. Of course you have to be sensible about how you choose to be stubborn. If you are stubborn in a close-minded way, it will not be to your advantage. If you are stubborn and you do not let anything get in the way of your greatest vision, you will make the vision breathe into life. Stubbornness is to have a strong will and stand point. If there is a will, there is a way. When you are stubborn, you will stand up for what you believe in regardless of if people agree or not. Stubbornness means not allowing your failures to tell you "no" but for your failures to tell you "try again." If you are not stubborn about your dream, it means that you do not want it bad enough. It means that you just kind of want your dream. If you want your dream bad enough, your stubbornness will prevent anything from destroying your dream and you will be actively working towards your dream every waking moment until you achieve it.

To love is to desire. You have to love your dream. When you love your dream, desire your dream, you will have the emotional motivation to chase it. If something does not make you feel emotionally stimulated and does not move you, the dream is not big enough. Your dream should give you a sense of fear. Through the fear, you will develop the courage to face your dream. What importance is your dream if it does not emotionally make you feel? Your dream will not have much purpose if it does not mentally make your brain smile in awe before you achieve it.

In my personal life, if something gives me the chills through my spine, butterflies in my gut, or lightheadedness while I'm thinking about it, I will forget about everything and only focus on working towards that dream. You have to make sacrifices and do things differently if you want to dance together with your dream. You have to love yourself, trust yourself, and feel that you deserve your dream. Once you have established that you are worthy of your dream then you must approach the dream.

Great dreams bring a great deal of pain before they are recognized. If you are not willing to undergo a great amount of pain, then you are not going to be subjected to experiencing the great amount of pleasure associated with living your dream. When the pain and destruction is great, the pleasure and evolution will be great. The pain you experience could be physical, psychological, emotional, or financial, for example.

If there is only pleasure in the journey of achieving your dream, you will not value the dream as much. The dream will be purposeless. Facing of a fear or fears is one great pain that many people are subjected to before their dream is achieved. Every time it hurts and you feel like you cannot go on, just remember that the only thing that stands between you and your dream is time. It is not the amount of pain or failure. It is only a matter of time. The more that you fail and experience pain, the more pleasurable the dream will be. Pain is the currency for buying pleasure.

Love is the greatest strength that you can extract from yourself. Love tells you that it is possible and that you must go on. Have a journal and mark down everything that you have done that got you one step closer to your dream. You will be surprised by the progress over time. Love is nurturing, love is caring, love believes, and love is true. Your love will give you the confidence to tackle any mountain in your life. Love is pleasure and love is peace. It hurts today, it hurts tomorrow, but it will never hurt forever. Pain is only temporary and temporary is only the pain.

The odds of you achieving your grandest dreams are not even a fraction of a percent of the odds of you being here today. The odds of you existing here today are approximately 1 in 400,000,000,000,000. The odds of you achieving your dream are 50/50. Either you are going to work and complete your dream, or you are going to be lazy and not complete your dream. Achieving your dream is binary. It mostly comes down to sheer laziness and the wrong story. If you want it, you will get it. Do not let anybody tell you that it is impossible to achieve your dream. It may be impossible for them, but it is not impossible for you. Your story is your story. Their story is their story. Your story in your mind has a way of telling your story in reality. If you do not like your story, or the story in your mind, change it. Most importantly, love the change and change to love. You are responsible for your life. You put the time, energy, discipline, commitment, and emotion into something.

If I can write, "I can do anything" then it means, "I can do anything." If I can write, "You can do anything" then it means, "You can do anything." If those two statements were untrue, a gravitational spiritual force would prevent me from writing those two statements down. If it were impossible, something would freeze me and make me backspace and take those two statements down. The fact that I was able to write those two statements means that if I can do anything, so can you.

The only person that puts limits on you is you. The only person that pushes your limits to the maximum is you. Whatever the limit you feel you have, push the limit a little higher. From there, push the limit a little higher. Raise your standards and push your limits. Push your limits until you feel that you can achieve the unlimited. Limits do nothing but make us barely succeed. Limits make us minimalists. When you put no limits on yourself, you will be able to exceed further than any limit that you have put on yourself before. Become a maximalist and achieve as high as you possibly can. The sky is your limit and the galaxy is your unlimited. Love yourself.

You are infinitely inwards and you are infinitely outwards. For the universe is greater than any sum. Understand the math and the math of loving yourself and you will be on your way. Life does not need to remain ordinary, it can become extraordinary. Anybody can do it. Success is not for a special breed. Whatever your definition of success is, you can achieve it!

My high school yearbook quote said,

"I believe that life gives you unlimited opportunities that may seem overwhelming, but if you look deep within, it is a blessing to realize how much potential a person can have. Anyone can make a difference with a positive outlook and willingness to put in the time to achieve a goal." (2013)
—Matt Petryga

Acknowledgments

I would like to acknowledge my mother and father, Dana and Donald. I love you both and you inspire me to live a purposeful life. I am thankful to both of you for giving me life, for all of the things that you have done for me, and for all of the valuable lessons that you have taught me.

I would also like to acknowledge my younger and only brother, Brandon. You inspire me to work hard and to be the best older brother that I can be to you. It has been and is still a great pleasure to watch you learn and to grow as a person that is kind and caring. You really are a gentle soul and I love you dearly.

There are too many other people who have brought positivity and joy into my life to name and you all deserve acknowledgement. You all know who you are, even if you were in my life momentarily.

Lastly, I would like to acknowledge you, the reader. You are the reason that I wake up and do the best that I can to give my talents and gifts to the world. I may know you personally or I may not know you at all, but regardless, I love you. I love you for being in the same universe as me. You serve a purpose on the same planet as me and I love you for living your own unique life, no matter how far it is that you may be. I wish you nothing but success, happiness, contentment, and peace in your life.

With great love,
—Matthew D. Petryga